Precious Lord, Take My Hand

MEDITATIONS

for CAREGIVERS

SHELLY BEACH

DISCOVERY HOUSE
PUBLISHERS®

Discovery House Publishers is affiliated with RBC Ministries, Grand Rapids, Michigan.

Discovery House books are distributed to the trade exclusively by Barbour Publishing, Inc., Uhrichsville, Ohio.

Requests for permission to quote from this book should be directed to: Permissions Department, Discovery House Publishers, P.O. Box 3566, Grand Rapids, MI 49501.

The title and lyrics of "Precious Lord, Take My Hand" are used by permission of Alfred Publishing Co., Inc., Van Nuys, CA.

Scripture quotations are from the *Holy Bible, New International Version®. NIV®.* Copyright ©1973, 1978, 1984 by Biblica, Inc.™ Used by permission of Zondervan. All rights reserved worldwide. www.zondervan.com

Interior design by Nicholas Richardson

Library of Congress Cataloging-in-Publication Data
Beach, Shelly.
    Precious Lord, take my hand : meditations for caregivers / Shelly Beach.
        p.   cm.
ISBN 978-1-57293-195-4
1. Caregivers—Religious life. 2. Caring—Religious aspects—Christianity. I. Title.
BV4910.9.B43   2007
242'.68—dc22   2007009353

Printed in the United States of America

10 11 12 13 14 / BPI / 12 11 10 9 8 7

To Dan,
love of my life,
my head,
my heart,
and my hero.

CONTENTS

A PERSPECTIVE FOR THE JOURNEY
An Overview of Our Caregiving Experience

The summer I was seven years old, my parents piled the family into our white Biscayne station wagon to go visit Aunt Evelyn and Uncle Arnie. They lived near Springfield, Illinois, which was seven hours from our home in Muskegon, Michigan.

It was a long road trip, made even longer by the fact that in those days travel often made me carsick. And since handy Zip-Loc bags had not been invented yet, my brother Paul often became a bit skittish about sitting in the same seat with me.

I remember lying in the back of our station wagon, working hard to ignore the motion of our behemoth family auto lumbering across endless interstates and winding back roads. With each hour and turn of the wheel, I became more viscerally aware of the intricacies of our route.

At one corner my father would turn right. At another, left. Occasionally I would peek bravely from my fetal position to the roadside scenes drifting past us, attuned to a strange sensation rising within me. Commensurate with the expanding knot in my stomach, my awe for my father was growing with each mile.

How could Dad possibly know the way? Out of all the roads in the United States, how did my father know precisely the right ones to choose? As the miles flew by, my amazement mounted. My father had to be a genius. The world was a tangle of lanes and highways, avenues and streets, but my father knew them all and could safely find our way.

When my husband, Dan, and I stepped into our caregiving role, I longed for the confidence of a father who knew every intricacy of the journey—who anticipated each turn on the horizon, who knew when to merge to the right or the left, who knew secret shortcuts. Instead, it seemed that one gray fall afternoon, Dan and I were asked to pull our battered and rusted Pinto onto a narrow path through a dense forest, without direction, headed toward an uncertain destination.

In that moment, the only thing we could do was look up to our heavenly Father, knowing that our direction through the tangle ahead must come from Him.

The Journey Begins: Norman and the Carson City, Michigan, Years

My husband, Dan, was serving as the administrator of a small Christian school in Carson City, Michigan, and I was the English Department when Dan's father, Norman, came to live with us for the first time. Our children were five and seven.

Extreme food allergies had narrowed Norman's food choices so severely that he'd become malnourished. As a widower living alone, his problems escalated to a crisis before we were aware of it. By the time his friends called from Missouri to report how truly ill he was, Norman was emaciated and unable to speak. Doctors feared he was dying of pancreatic cancer.

We were able to find good medical care for Norman and plump him up again to return home after four months. But several years later, food allergies again brought him to the brink of starvation. We were still living in Carson City, and once again he came to live with us as we sought a complete medical assessment. Once again we renourished his body, and after six months Norman returned to his home in Missouri. Dan and I thought our caregiving work was complete. Dad Beach seemed healthy again. What we didn't realize was that symptoms of depression were beginning to mark his life.

Motion Sickness: My Illness and the Mt. Pleasant Years

Not long after Dad Beach returned to Missouri, Dan and I accepted positions at a Christian school in Mt. Pleasant, Michigan, just two hours from my parents' home in Muskegon. We would serve this school for ten years. During those years, family members began to detect changes in my mother, and it became increasingly clear that she had dementia. Our hearts sank as we watched symptoms progress. Dad spoke of the difficulties she was experiencing, but like most caregivers, he sheltered us from the true extent of her struggles.

It was during our years in Mt. Pleasant, in 1999, that I became ill with a walnut-sized, non-tumorous brain lesion near my brain stem. The experience changed my life forever. After steroid treatment, the lesion shrunk, leaving me with atypical migraines and a cluster of neurological symptoms that still keep doctors shaking their heads. But I recovered my abilities to walk and see and read—all gifts lost for a time. Over the next few years, I would slowly improve, then plateau, and since on most days I now generally know which end of the fork to stick in my mouth, I consider myself abundantly blessed.

It was also while we were living in Mt. Pleasant that Dan and I, along with my brother Paul and his wife Sheryl, began to transition into caregiving roles for my parents.

Brambles and Thickets: The Iowa Years

In the fall of 2000, Dan and I felt God leading us to take positions at a Christian school in Iowa. The move was not easy for me, as it took us so far from Mom and Dad. We would spend the next four years in Waterloo, Iowa. During those years, Norman went into a full medical and mental crisis in Missouri, and we moved him in and out of medical facilities, as the particular crisis of the moment dictated, and then permanently into our home. While we were helping Norman with his profound health issues, my father's health began to fail, my mother's Alzheimer's went galloping full-steam ahead, the prodigal son we had left behind in Michigan moved out to live with us in Iowa, and our daughter, who had been at college and then on the mission field, moved home. During this same four-year period, Dan was hospitalized five times, and, not to be outdone, I was in and out of emergency rooms a few times myself.

Mom's needs were escalating, and Dad was under extreme pressure caring for her alone. I was making emergency medical trips between Iowa and Michigan on a regular basis. Our friends couldn't keep up with the stream of medical appointments and crises we were managing. At times, neither could we.

After four years in Iowa, where we were blessed with

fabulous care to get Norman stabilized, we moved back to Michigan, leaving both our adult children behind.

The Clearing: The Return to Michigan

We were able to keep Norman with us in our home in Michigan for four months before it became clear that his Parkinson's Disease had compromised his balance to the point where he couldn't be left alone for any length of time. We transitioned him into a veteran's facility just a few miles from our home, where he died eight months later. Shortly after our return to Michigan, Mom and Dad came to live with Dan and me and with my brother Paul and his wife Sheryl, in a shared arrangement. They continue to do so at this writing.

Eternal Perspective: The View from Above

These years of caregiving have involved both a journey and a change of perspective. That change of perspective has come in bits and pieces as we traveled from the old into the new, and as we found our way through brambles and thickets. Along the way, I have learned that even though the world is a tangle of paths and highways, avenues and streets, my Father knows them all, so we needn't fear finding our way.

My family is on a journey together, and whether or not we're skittish about seating arrangements, we're confident we're heading toward a pre-determined destination. My earthly father has relinquished the driver's seat, but he is confident, as we are, that our Father knows each turn on the horizon and the secret shortcuts.

Our perspective is eternal—a view from above.

> *"For I know the plans I have for you," declares the Lord, "plans to prosper you and not to harm you, plans to give you hope and a future. Then you will call upon me and come and pray to me, and I will listen to you. You will seek me and find me when you seek me with all your heart." —Jeremiah 29:11–13*

INTRODUCTION

I told myself it would be a simple task, but I couldn't bring myself to do it.

I sat on the floor of my living room, staring blankly at the music books fanned out in piles encircling me. *Songs Everybody Loves, Duets and Trios, Favorites Number One, Favorites Number Two . . .* different titles, but all bearing one distinct similarity. On the cover of each, in curling, graceful script, a name had been penned in the top right-hand corner.

The name of my mother, whose velvety voice had graced listeners over five decades in churches, at rallies, and over the airwaves in the heyday of live radio. My mother, who taught me to draw sweet harmonies out of the air before I knew what a musical note looked like. My mother, who was slipping into the shadows of Alzheimer's disease and whose needs were drawing me home to hold her hand on the journey.

As I reminisced over the stacks of books before me that summer afternoon in 2004, I knew I had to let them go. There would simply not be enough room in our new home in Michigan for the dozens of titles that bore my mother's markings.

During the weeks of packing, I spent hours culling through them, fingering the pages as the melodies played through my head. *His eye is on the sparrow . . . Nothing between my soul and the Savior . . . I come to the garden alone . . . .* For days the music drifted through my thoughts as I stacked boxes for the move from Iowa to Michigan. And for days the books remained in uneven piles on the living room floor as I deferred the inevitable. My husband Dan—wise, gracious, and a man of few words—said nothing and simply walked around the scattered stacks.

On a hot July afternoon I knelt on the living room floor for the last time, a plastic grocery bag beside me and a craft knife in my hand. Dan would come after I had finished my task and place the remaining books in the trash. I quickly slid a half dozen choices into the sack, then carefully razored a song I had known to be my mother's favorite from one of the books and slipped it inside a file folder. That past Christmas, on an evening when even my name had slipped behind the clouds of Mom's memory, she had sung every word of it with the family as we sat at the piano at Paul and Sheryl's.

Precious Lord, take my hand,
Lead me on, help me stand,
I am tired, I am weak, I am worn.
Through the storm, through the night,
Lead me on to the light,
Take my hand, precious Lord,
Lead me home.

In the months since Christmas, the song had wedged its way into my heart as I watched Mom's descent into the thickening mist of Alzheimer's. The words had become my plea for the presence of God to overwhelm her in the growing darkness. The words were my prayer for my brother Paul and his wife Sheryl who had joined hands with my husband Dan and me as caregivers. They were my entreaty for my father as he watched the ravages of disease smother his wife's mind as he quietly faced his own physical losses.

Over the next months and years, the sweet melody of this song would sooth Mom to sleep in the difficult night hours when her mind was most tormented. It became the prayer that wove itself into the fabric of my life as Dan and I, Paul and Sheryl cared for Mom and Dad. It spoke hope when I felt hopeless and gave voice to my broken heart that often could find no words of its own.

Christmas of 2004 we exchanged only token gifts as a family. We were gathered at my brother Paul's house—

Grandma, Grandpa, aunts and uncles, cousins, brothers and sisters. Dan and I were now less than an hour from my parents' home and overseeing needs that seemed to be spiraling downward. Their future with us seemed tenuous, and the health challenges that Paul, Sheryl, Dan, and I all faced had transitioned from worrisome to daunting. Being together was gift enough, we had all concurred.

But the need to give one gift compelled me. It was a gift for my brother Paul, but as much a gift for my own heart. A matted, framed, and faded copy of *Precious Lord, Take My Hand.* It was more than a sentimental memento. The gift represented my desire to razor truth from a musty book and set it in a gilt frame in a place of prominence in my heart.

Precious Lord, You hold our hands.

You lead us on and give us grace to stand when we are tired, weak, and worn.

No matter the storm or the night, You lead us on to the light.

You hold our hands, Precious Lord.

Lead us home.

The faded music bearing my mother's breath marks and underlinings sits atop Paul and Sheryl's piano in their dining room. But its truth has wound itself around my heart, binding hope there in the velvety tones of my mother's voice.

Precious Lord, Take My Hand

Search me, O God, and know my heart;
test me and know my anxious thoughts.
See if there is any offensive way in me,
and lead me in the way everlasting.

PSALM 139:23–24

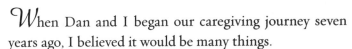

*W*hen Dan and I began our caregiving journey seven years ago, I believed it would be many things.

I believed it would be a timeline of events with a beginning, a middle, and an end.

I believed it would consist of acts of care, service, and sacrifice.

I believed it would be a time of ministering to our loved ones, perhaps set to a soundtrack resembling strains from *Little House on the Prairie*.

And while these things were true, except that the soundtrack sounded more like music from *Diary of a Mad Housewife*, I was to discover startling things about caregiving that knocked me off balance and left me breathless, as though I had been caught unexpectedly in a sudden summer shower.

I did not expect the work of caregiving to come wrapped in the trappings of my childhood, in my compulsions to please others, to be thought of as the good daughter, and to keep the affairs of my entire family in well-ordered balance like the plate-spinner at the circus.

I did not expect caregiving to expose wounds at the center of my being, where my identity had been shaped as a child and I had named myself *Unworthy* and *Unloved.*

I did not expect caregiving to be about childhood roles and hurts that had carried into adulthood and hidden themselves like dust bunnies behind the family refrigerator.

I did not expect caregiving to be a mirror that reflected my own broken image of myself. And I did not expect caregiving to be a path of restoration for my own heart and a journey of redemption in my relationships with others.

What I expected and what I got in my caregiving experiences were two entirely different things. Praise God.

What He gave me was the soul-searching opportunity to journey back into my childhood and find my true identity in Christ. He gave me the privilege of re-shaping my relationship with those around me as I learned to establish healthy boundaries and a foundation of respect. He granted me new vision for those I love, and with that new vision, a new sense of compassion and grace.

The work of caregiving should be reserved for the truly courageous or the blindly naive. It is soul-crunching, spirit-bending, body-wearying work because it is redemptive work. In caregiving we reflect Christ's love: unconditional love, unequivocal love, unreserved love. We are called to love in ways that will either change us or break us.

The day that Dan and I began our caregiving journey, we linked arms and plunged off a cliff. We didn't know that the hardest tasks we would face would be to allow our hearts to be molded, to be searched, and to allow God to use this special time to conform us to His image in new ways. On days when I felt I was plunging toward earth in an out-of-control freefall, God showed me my agendas, my reservations, my fears, my vanities, my pride, my selfishness. He used my infirmities to show me His sufficiency.

My pastor has said, "The best day is the day you see yourself for who you are, desperate without Christ, then see yourself as He sees you, complete in Him." This was the blessing of caregiving in my life. As I saw who God had created me to be, I turned and ran weeping into His arms.

This is my prayer for you—that as you see yourself in the days ahead, that you, too, turn and run weeping into the open arms of God.

Dear gracious Father, may we recognize today our desperate need of You, that You are the source of all love, wisdom, and grace. We confess that we are wounded and broken, in need of Your love and forgiveness. I ask for Your forgiveness for my sin and for Your restoration of the broken places in my spirit. Search me and know my heart. Expose my anxious thoughts and offensive ways. You know my broken places so well, and You desire to see me whole. Pour out Your grace and mercy in my life like a healing balm.

ARE THERE WOUNDED places in your heart that God has revealed to you? What do you believe are God's desires for healing these wounds in your life? What areas of your life do you believe God may desire to reshape?

_____

_____

_____

_____

_____

_____

_____

_____

_____

_____

_____

_____

Praise the Lord, O my soul;
all my inmost being, praise his holy name . . .
and forget not all his benefits—
who forgives all your sins and heals all your diseases,
who redeems your life from the pit
and crowns you with love and compassion,
who satisfies your desires with good things
so that your youth is renewed like the eagle's.

PSALM 103:1–5

𝒪ur transition to Iowa was less than smooth, to say the least. It would be weeks before Dan and I could move into our new house, and so we settled into a pea-sized cabin at a picturesque Bible conference grounds. But within forty-eight hours of our arrival on Iowa soil, Dan's leg became hot and feverish and swelled to the size of a watermelon, and he was rushed off to the hospital with a case of raging cellulitis.

Because Dan and I were to work together as administrators at a Christian school and he was delirious and no longer knew his name, the task of new teacher orientation was left to me. So I spent my first days in Iowa orienting teachers whose names I didn't know to policies I didn't know at a school whose students I didn't know. It was not a happy week. I wanted Dan *well* and out of that hospital, and it really didn't have a whole lot to do with his cellulitis.

To be closer to the school and closer to the hospital, I temporarily abandoned our cabin at the Bible conference and moved in with a woman on the school board who had offered me a room in her spacious condo. Not being a dog lover, she was not as welcoming to our precious miniature dachshund, Beanie Weenie, who was sent off to live with a family from the school. Beanie did not react well to the Iowa move or the campground move or the condo move or the move to the school family and responded by taking on a new personality that soon qualified her for free short-term housing at the animal shelter.

There I was, living with a woman I barely knew and making daily visits to my delirious husband and my maniacal dog and failing miserably at juggling the administrative tasks of the school when all I really wanted to do was *go home* and *be alone* and close the door on the world.

So three months later, when both Dan and the dog had

returned to normal and with the keys to my new house in hand, I took up nesting with a Capital N. I finally had a space to call my own, and I wasn't in much of a mood for sharing.

Then the call came that Dan's father, Norman, was sick, really sick. It was a call that made me gulp hard. I cried. I may have even hidden in the closet for an hour or two. I never for a moment doubted that I would eventually choose to do the right thing, but I was pretty sure that doing the right thing was going to be an endurance test.

In the twenty-five years Dan and I had been married, we'd always been taking care of someone. We *deserved* a little time to ourselves, didn't we? I secretly harbored that thought, only allowing it to peek out briefly among friends I knew would sympathize. After all, Norman had lived with us twice before for extended periods of time. I knew if he returned I would lose elements of my privacy too difficult to even speak of. I knew I would lose the freedom to have friends over. I knew the weight of Norman's medical appointments would fall to me. I knew that the strain on our marriage would be enormous, and that our caregiving would become the greatest frustration in our relationship. I knew Norman's presence would impact our finances, our vacations, our children, our sex life, our health, our jobs, and every decision regarding our future.

It was a weighty decision, yet it was a right decision,

and at the core of my being I knew it. Yet I struggled with resentment.

Ultimately, resentment boils down to one thing: our belief that God isn't giving us what we deserve. We think we should be getting something better. It's a direct attack on God's sovereignty, much like the argument Satan used on Eve in the Garden: *God doesn't really want what's best for You. He's withholding the really good stuff.*

Resentment starts with the lie that I have a right to my own life. The truth of the matter is, if I'm a child of God, I'm all His.

My bad attitude always boils down to lies. Living a life of faith always means resting in truth. The battle against resentment is fought with the weapon of God's Truth, one lie at a time, one moment at a time.

Dear gracious and loving Lord, forgive me for the resentment that I so often harbor. I look at circumstances and judge them according to what I think is fair. Father, help me to trust You to judge all things. I thank You today for the many good things that You have poured out in my life. They all belong to You, and I hold them in my hand freely as an offering. May Your Holy Spirit reveal the resentment in my life and show me the truth from Your Word that will release me to live in freedom and joy.

HAVE YOU STRUGGLED with what seems "fair" in your caregiving? Is it difficult for you to entrust those things to God? What steps can you take to help you expose the lies that bind you in this area?

_____

_____

_____

_____

_____

_____

_____

_____

_____

_____

By day the Lord went ahead of them in a pillar of
cloud to guide them on their way
and by night in a pillar of fire to give them light,
so that they could travel by day or night.

EXODUS 13:21

God dragged me from Michigan to Iowa, kicking and screaming. Of course, the kicking and screaming weren't my fault. At least that's what I told myself. God was asking me to leave people behind who really needed me—people who depended on me for their care.

Like my mom, who was slipping into the grip of Alzheimer's.

And my dad, who had a bad heart and was having cardiac episodes so often that the ER nurses were thinking of inviting him to their Tupperware parties.

And Alicia, whose mother was my dear friend. By the age of eight, Alicia had undergone forty brain surgeries, not counting the operations on her body below the neck.

And other family members who had so many health anomalies that we could have had a section of a medical textbook with our name on it.

So it was perfectly obvious to me that I had every right to kick and scream as I crossed the Old Muddy and headed into corn country. God didn't seem to be aware that *He needed me* in Michigan doing things that seemed far more important than whatever He intended for me to do when we got to Iowa.

But before Dan and I had packed our first box, God had set His plan in place. Of course we were deaf to the thrummings of the cords in the tapestry humming about our ears—countless cords being spun with the promise and brilliance of eternity. But in slivers of time over the years, God has let us hear the rhythm and the lilt of the weaving, like a hummingbird darting in close, then flitting away.

We were unaware of the movement of the Weaver's hands as hundreds of miles away Dan's father began to fall ill, even as we began to pack our first boxes. Norman himself barely realized he was getting sick.

It was months later, in the days after he had moved in with us and we began to look for support services to care for his challenging physical and mental health needs, that we fully realized what moving to Iowa had meant.

Unknowingly, we had selected a home in the state, the county, and the city where Norman could receive the best care in the country and we could receive the best possible family support services. God had also gifted us with a five-bedroom, three-bath home, knowing we would need a suite of rooms for Dad Beach. God had gone before us and moved us to a place of refuge and provision for Dan's father.

The day that Dan and I crossed the Iowa state line, however, I wept openly for the things I was leaving behind. I did not realize I was stepping into my future and my hope.

You go ahead of me. That is the message of God's sufficiency to those of us who are kickers and screamers. It is what stills us and silences us—the knowledge that God has already provided all that we need, and more, before we even know how to ask.

> *Gracious Lord, You are so patient with my fits and tantrums, my pride and my self-centeredness. Forgive me for my self-will and lack of trust. Remind me that what I see is not what I get, and that You go before me and behind me, surrounding me at every turn with Your purposes in all things. May I rest in this truth.*

HAVE YOU EVER kicked and screamed and found that God has gone ahead of you and prepared the way? How has this increased your faith?

_____

_____

_____

_____

_____

_____

_____

_____

_____

_____

But the plans of the Lord stand firm forever,
the purposes of his heart through all generations.

PSALM 33:11

$\mathcal{I}$t's the fall of 2000, and calls have been coming to our Iowa home from people in Missouri we barely know. I hand the phone to Dan and watch him scavenge his brain for identities to match the names of people from the church his father has attended for years. We've met few of Dad Beach's friends in the fifteen years he's lived in Missouri. Our visits there have been few and far between. From the time our children were born, Dad always came to visit Dan and me in Michigan, and later in Iowa, and then driving on to visit Dan's sister Sue and her husband Jeff in New York. It was his annual circuit driving tour after finishing up his ministry with Child Evangelism at the summer fairs of Missouri, a missionary ministry he began at the age of sixty-four when he moved there from New York after his wife died.

Dan and I made one visit to Dad's Missouri home in a cold January when our youngest, Nathan, was a month old. We'd left his older sister, Jessica, with Grandma and Grandpa Burke, knowing that a house under construction was no place for a toddler. Dad Beach had purchased the house from the estate of a ninety-year-old woman who had died in her rocking chair in front of the wood-burning stove she had stoked herself until the day she died. The accommodations were spartan in those days, but, then, austerity had always been Norman's way of life. The miniscule house had no insulation, no interior walls, and no running water. The outhouse leaned to the south at a forty-five degree angle, and each time I used it, I was certain I was going to plunge into its depths. Wells came at a price in that part of Missouri, and Dad had chosen to hold out until city water came down his road. It would be eleven long years in coming, but if it seemed a long time to Dad Beach, he wasn't mentioning it.

Dad's best friend was Ron. The two men had spent hours jacking up the basement of the tiny house, replacing windows, nailing on new shingles, and rebuilding the place from the ground up. Decades separated the two men in age. Worlds separated them in life experience, yet they were bonded in an enigmatic way that intrigued us as children and, frankly, left us a bit envious.

When we think of those calls from Missouri, we remember the intensity of Ron's voice—the voice of someone who cared deeply for his friend. Something just wasn't quite right with Norm, he said. He wasn't coming to church or answering his phone. Ron seemed convinced that it would be best if we came down and checked to be sure everything was all right. Norm just didn't seem to be *himself.*

We'd sensed it ourselves in Dad Beach's voice in recent phone calls. The long pauses. The cryptic answers. It was too familiar. He had been sick twice before—deathly sick, emaciated and silent; and both times Dan had driven the long trip to bring him back to live with us for months until he was well enough to be alone again. But this time Dad was seventy-nine years old. Dan and I both knew that when Dad Beach came to us this time to recuperate, he might never be strong enough to live alone again.

Sometimes God does not give us time to think deeply about life-changing decisions. Sometimes He only allows us to respond at the visceral level, where truth and faith abide. Perhaps it's because He realizes that time spent thinking about eventualities and possibilities is time lost to the pursuit of greater things.

Our journey to Missouri that fall changed our lives forever. The empty nest we envisioned in Iowa was full by Christmas. Norman moved into our home on a permanent basis, in a whirlwind of packing and paperwork. Weeks later, our son Nathan arrived, a prodigal seeking restoration. Nathan took up occupancy in our basement, and Norman settled into rooms just down the hallway from our bedroom.

From the foundations of the earth, God had ordained the day that a son and, eventually, a daughter would return to our home and the day that a father would return to us. His plan and His purpose were to allow our family a window of time to share a home and a heritage, and to fulfill the desires of His heart for generations to come.

It would be years before we would see the fruit of our decision. But the fruit would come as God ministered spiritual healing and reconciliation in the lives of three generations one day at a time for the next four years.

Dear God, what a blessing to think that my work of caregiving will influence generations to come. I sit in a place of honor and influence, and I do not take that responsibility lightly. Thank You for the opportunity to minister to future generations by ministering to family members in this way. Lord, help me to remember that before the foundations of the earth, You have ordained Your purposes for our lives. May I take joy in that, despite the difficulties that I may face today.

HOW HAS CAREGIVING for your loved ones influenced your life and the lives of your family members? Did you care for an elderly grandparent in your home? What are some of the positive generational influences of your caregiving?

_____

_____

_____

_____

_____

_____

_____

_____

_____

_____

A fool gives full vent to his anger,
but a wise man keeps himself under control .

$\mathcal{T}$he neighbors probably think I'm crazy. It wouldn't be the first time, and it won't be the last.

I am standing in the driveway with a garden shovel clutched in my hands, whacking wildly at a clump of ice that has formed beneath a corner gutter. With each smack, I am uttering prayers with a volume and stridency that should cause anyone on the block with an iota of sense to gather their children and lock their doors.

My prayers consist of variations on only a few words which I am speaking with an intensity that borders on mania.

"I can't do this."

"You can't expect me to do this."

"I do not have the strength to do this."

With each sentence, I hew into the ice mound like a Paul Bunyan on steroids. A searing pain rips through my chest, and later that weekend the ER doc will tell me that I have ripped the ligaments in my chest away from my sternum. This from a menopausal woman who can barely make it through her *Curves* workout.

It's amazing what anger can do. And I don't think the ice felt a thing.

That moment of indignation is burned clearly into my memory—indignation that God could expect me to carry such a heavy burden when I simply didn't have enough strength for the load. Indignation that He would ask me to do something so difficult. After all, He loved me and had a wonderful plan for my life, right?

The truth was, my anger was really a pity party wrapped around a bundle of lies.

I deserve better than this.

God isn't enough after all.

Nobody cares anyway.

These were my lies on that given day. I had developed creative variations for other days.

To say that I did not find myself startled by anger, especially in the early months of my caregiving, would be a lie. The refreshing reality was that God was not startled by my anger. He knew the weak places in my heart, the places that needed some rooting around, where the soil had grown fallow. He knew the lies that lay submerged beneath the surface of my soul, just out of view, and He chose, in His love and mercy, to excavate them with pain and a garden shovel.

Satan has a standard repertoire for all of us, and we'll all face our Paul Bunyan moments of anger in caregiving. Sometimes our anger will be born out of righteousness, but most often it will be a pity party wrapped around a bundle of lies. Your temper tantrum may not involve a garden shovel, but it will have the same power to sear your soul. It will scar you from the inside out, where the wounds will be hardest for you to see.

People who choose to cling to their anger become mired in the trap of bitterness, never moving forward. Despite their floundering and straining, they are bound to the place where their anger first gripped them. And the only antidote for anger is truth.

The truth is, God in His mercy did not give me what I deserve; He gave me mercy instead.

The truth is that God is more than enough, despite what I see.

The truth is that His strength is sufficient. But I must choose to lay down the shovel and take Jesus' hand extended in mercy and grace.

The truth is that God is big enough to listen to my anger but loving enough to show me the path of truth beyond it that leads to wisdom.

Dear gracious and loving Lord, forgive me for my outbursts of anger. So often they are centered on what I want and what I see, and those things are often painful and hard. You have promised me sufficiency in all things, and I claim that truth in my life today, knowing that Your strength is made perfect in weakness. Expose my sinful anger and root it out of my life, dear Lord. Today I choose to lay down my sinful anger and accept Your mercy and grace. Thank You for forgiveness and for truth that leads to wisdom.

HOW HAVE YOU struggled with anger? What areas of anger is God asking you to lay aside? What steps of repentance and restoration do you feel God may be asking you to take regarding anger?

_____

_____

_____

_____

_____

_____

_____

_____

_____

_____

I know that you can do all things;
no plan of yours can be thwarted.

JOB 42:2

𝒯he signs were there for years, but we were reluctant to read them. We all knew, at some deep level, that something was wrong with Mom. But to speak the lurking suspicions out loud gave them power to become reality, and none of us wanted to be the first to give our fears a voice. Perhaps we felt we could keep them powerless if they remained unnamed.

At first we observed idiosyncrasies and behaviors that grew slowly into caricatures and obsessions. Small things, oddities, we told ourselves. But behind closed doors, when Dan and I would visit Mom and Dad, we would raise our eyebrows at Mom's bedtime routine, always precisely the same.

"Do you need anything? More blankets?"

"No, Mom. We're fine."

"Okay, then. I'll just check a few things."

She would wander from the family room where Dan and I would linger watching TV after she and Dad had gone to bed, meandering through the house, randomly opening and closing doors, eventually returning to begin the questioning again.

"Do you need anything? More blankets?"

"No, Mom."

And the routine would repeat itself.

Other things began to change as well. Her usual meticulous appearance took on a rather ragamuffin look. Her clothes were often stained or unkempt. Dad had taken responsibility for the laundry, mentioning that the basement seemed to frighten Mom and he had found her crying down there one day because she couldn't find her way back up the stairs. She developed an obsession for Mentos, Kleenexes, and purses, and for several years we never left the house without a purse stuffed with tissues and mints.

By the time my niece Keri graduated from high school, we all suspected that Mom was struggling with dementia. Keri's party pretty much put the icing on the cake. We didn't discover the problem until guests began to leave, and the women couldn't find their purses. Mom, thinking the handbags scattered about the house were all hers, had hidden them all for safekeeping. Some in the dryer. Some in the clothes hamper. Some in closets. Some under beds. (We now can attest to the fact that whether it's purses or jewelry or her own clothing, Mom's skill in hiding things can baffle the best of us.)

It's never been easy for my family to sit down and work through plans for our parents' care in a neatly wrapped package. If that is any family's experience, I have yet to meet them. It is hard work to recognize needs, name them, then move forward as a family unit with the courage and forethought to devise a plan and then to implement it. But the day we admitted that Mom had a problem was the day that we could begin discussing how to help her. We needed to figure out what love and support looked like and how we could help provide it for her and my father.

God's plan for my mother did not end when her dementia began. His plan for her is eternal, and in embracing a plan for her health needs, we are embracing His plan for her at this stage of her life. My mother's journey through Alzheimer's is as sacred as her years of parenting her children or caregiving for her own sister.

This is Dan's and my calling right now—a calling to walk beside my mom, dad, and Norman in a stage of their life that God has marked out for them, at a stage of our lives where God has enabled us to do so. This is not a path that all children or family members can walk or will walk in the same way, and God never intended for it to be. He only asks us to walk with confidence the separate paths He lights before us.

Dear God, it is so difficult to admit and accept the difficulties in our lives—diagnoses, deaths, losses, wounds. Sometimes we squeeze our eyes shut and refuse to admit that they are there. But You have promised to be with us in all things, and it is as we embrace the truth that You can be glorified and we can join You in Your plan for our future. Give me grace to face the difficult things today and a heart to speak Your praise in the midst of it.

WHAT TRUTHS HAVE you been forced to face that have been difficult for you? How has God shown Himself to you in these circumstances? How have the people of God ministered to you in these times?

_____

_____

_____

_____

_____

_____

_____

_____

_____

Fear not, for I have redeemed you;
I have summoned you by name; you are mine . . .
everyone who is called by my name, whom I created for my glory,
whom I formed and made.

ISAIAH 43:1, 7

*F*ear takes many forms for the caregiver. The look on the doctor's face as he rounds a corner. The social worker's slow intake of breath before speaking an inevitable truth you wish to deny. The knowing look in the eyes of a friend who sees the difficult path before you—a friend who takes your hand, giving you strength for the first step.

Carmen is one such friend. She, too, rides motorcycles and shares an aversion to helmets. She, too, is a teacher and shares a passion for kids. And she, too, cares for a beloved family member in her home—her grandmother.

In the early months of our friendship, Carmen and I talked long and often. Her grandmother struggles with a neurological disease that parallels Dan's father's illness. Carmen and I stepped into the role of caregivers side-by-side as we simultaneously transitioned our loved ones into our homes. We shared the same social worker and swapped stories about commodes, shower chairs, and podiatrists. We vented over Snickers bars about the insanity of our lives—juggling caregiving, teaching, church involvement, and home. We laughed whenever we could and as long as we could, and sometimes we cried. Me more often than Carmen. She is built for marathons, and on the hard days I would step behind her and feel myself drawn forward in the power of her wake.

Within months of meeting Carmen, conversations shifted to my parents' needs. My calls home became more frequent as Dad reported Mom's increasingly odd behavior. Confusion, angry outbursts, insomnia, wandering, irrationality. I read the bewilderment and desperation in my father's tone and wouldn't allow myself to voice the thoughts that raced through my head. As I spoke to Carmen during those days, I chose my words carefully. My lips were not yet ready to speak into existence the truth I already knew. But Carmen heard what I could not bring myself to say.

On a November afternoon she stepped into my office and placed a book in my hands. Few words passed between us before she turned and left. The book lay on my desk for days before I found the courage to open it.

The Mayo Clinic Book on Alzheimer's.

I didn't want to see my mother in its pages. I didn't want to acknowledge the path that lay ahead for her, for my father, for our entire family. The very title struck fear in my heart, fear I didn't want to face. My mother had Alzheimer's.

At times pain overwhelms truth. But God's truth always overcomes, whether or not we see it or understand it. As I opened the pages of the book, I came face to face with a truth I already knew, a truth that had existed before the foundations of time. My mother had Alzheimer's, and God had permitted it.

A second book gave me the grace to accept it. Through the words of Scripture, God whispered to my heart that I had no reason to fear. He Himself had summoned my mother by name. He had formed and shaped her. He would work out the details of her life, even a life with Alzheimer's, for His glory and her good. He had summoned my mother down a path we would not choose. But it was a path He had marked, and He would be there for each step.

I eventually picked up the book Carmen gave me and read it cover to cover. I learned a lot from its pages, and not just about Alzheimer's. I learned that fear can be vanquished in even the simplest of acts of faith, and that the faith to move forward can sometimes be borrowed from a friend.

Father God, help me to walk in Your truth, and for that truth to transform what I believe, even when the road ahead seems excruciatingly difficult. May my focus be on who You are and not the circumstances around me. You have summoned me, You have redeemed me, and I rest in Your character and Your love for me.

WHAT FEARS HAVE you faced as a caregiver? What truth from God's Word can help you transform these fears?

_____

_____

_____

_____

_____

_____

_____

_____

_____

_____

I thank Christ Jesus our Lord,
who has given me strength,
that he considered me faithful,
appointing me to his service.

1 TIMOTHY 1:12

$\mathcal{I}$ am visiting my parents for the weekend. I've made so many emergency medical flights back to Michigan in the few years we've lived in Iowa that the pilots at the Cedar Falls airport know my age, my real hair color, and how many kidney stones Dan has passed since we moved from Michigan.

This trip began with a phone conversation with my father. We were chatting along casually about the value of graham crackers purchased at Dollar General versus the value of graham crackers purchased at Aldi, when suddenly Dad was gone. I couldn't tell if he had passed out or had become distracted by the excitement of the mailman's arrival, but in a few minutes his voice returned, unintelligible and garbled. From my kitchen in Iowa it was difficult to determine if he was having a stroke or if eating the thirteen-year-old honey he kept in the basement had caught up with him.

So I pulled out my cell phone and called a neighbor with my left ear while I kept Dad on the phone with my right ear. The fact that I only had one mouth left them both a bit confused. But somehow Dad managed to get delivered to the ER, and I was off to Michigan, flying the friendly skies while I scarfed down Dramamine and Tums.

And, once again, Dan was left alone at home to cope with his father's spiraling health needs, not to mention his own mounting tensions at work. It didn't feel right for me to stay at home and ignore my dad's needs, and it didn't feel right for me to leave Dan. In spite of the fact that I can pinch a good deal more than an inch, there simply wasn't enough of me to go around.

Dad's emergency room visit turned up nothing. Over the years, his symptoms have been a bizarre collection of episodes that resemble strokes, heart attacks, seizures, and geriatric interpretations of The Mashed Potato. At times his ability to speak instantaneously disappears and his ability to read evaporates. Sometimes he trembles and spasms so severely that doctors have labeled him epileptic, only to reverse their opinion later. Other doctors have been convinced he needs open heart surgery or suffers from pulmonary insufficiency. He has seen specialists from one side of the state to the other, all of whom have agreed that he is a baffling case and have billed us anyway.

For years life has been a series of crisis interventions, as Paul, Sheryl, Dan, and I have driven, flown, and sped by whatever means possible to be present for procedures, consultations, emergency room visits for Dad and Mom. And for years I dealt with guilt for living out of state, for not being able to be there for everything, and fearing that I wouldn't be able to be with Mom and Dad at the moment when they might need me most.

But God never intended for me to live under that weight of guilt. His intent for me is to thank and praise Him for the things I can do and to pray and trust Him for the things I cannot do. This is the essence of faith, and it is hard. But this attitude adjustment has freed me to see that my glass each and every day is not half empty or half full, but overflowing because God has orchestrated the details of my days.

The reality of that truth has freed me from the enormity of guilt that threatens to overwhelm me. I cannot be all things to the people I love. I cannot be there for every procedure, every appointment, every difficulty. I cannot beat back the ravages of Alzheimer's. God has promised to give me the strength to be a servant, one day at a time. And He has reserved the role of Savior for Himself.

Dear Father, thank You for orchestrating the events of this day. You have laid out for me the privileges of servanthood, knowing that I cannot be all things to all people, and that You have reserved that role for Yourself. Thank You for the opportunities that I have had today to minister to my loved ones in whatever eternal role You had for me to play. Give me peace in knowing that I am touching eternity today, Father, whether that role is at the side of my loved one or separated from them at this moment in time.

HOW HAVE YOU BATTLED with the temptation to shoulder responsibility for everyone's well-being? How do you balance faithfulness in your servanthood with dependence upon Jesus Christ?

_____

_____

_____

_____

_____

_____

_____

_____

_____

_____

There is a time for everything,
and a season for every activity under heaven . . .
A time to weep and a time to laugh,
a time to mourn and a time to dance.

ECCLESIASTES 3:1, 4

Lucy has failed me. Mom has once again wandered away from the black and white images that flash from the screen accompanied by staccato laughter. She makes her way through the kitchen and down the hallway, following the voices that beckon her with words we cannot hear.

Exhausted, I lie on the family room couch where I have kept vigil, watching to make sure that her wanderings don't take her toward the door and into the dark of night. Dad is resting down the hall—his first real rest in months. Like most spouses of those suffering with Alzheimer's, he has let us see only the fraying edges of the problem. He hasn't had a full night's sleep in months.

Mom opens the doorway to the first bedroom and steps inside. I hear the closet door as she slides it open, and I envision her fingering the clothes. I hear the closet slide shut, and she slips back into the hallway and shuffles toward the next bedroom.

I close my eyes for a moment, knowing she will return. I decide to settle her on the couch beside me and orchestrate another interlude of distraction. Perhaps Lucy and Ethel will capture her attention, and I will be gifted with her laughter. Or perhaps she will rest her head on my shoulder and fall into the sleep I pray will give her respite from the shroud of confusion that tightens its stranglehold on her mind more and more each day.

I hear her footsteps in the hallway and open my eyes. She is standing in the family room doorway, staring down at her chest, her pink chiffon blouse discarded and a faded floral cobbler's apron in its place, the snaps unsecured. In each hand she gently cups a breast.

"Are these mine?" she asks, seemingly amazed that such accoutrements could belong to her.

I struggle to keep my face solemn and my voice matter-of-fact.

"Yes, Mom."

"Is there one on each side?"

"Yes, Mom," I repeat, not trusting myself to say more.

"Good, then. I'm just trying to get everything organized."

For a moment I find myself speechless. Nothing in my usual repertoire of responses fits this scenario. I finally manage to find my voice.

"Everything's right where it should be," I assure her.

"I hope so."

I settle her beside me on the couch. Raucous laughter draws her attention, and for another brief interlude she's with Ethel and Lucy.

The laughter draws me back as well—back to summers at the lake with family and friends. The children bundled off to bed on the screened porch overlooking the lake while the adults cluster around tables in the kitchen playing Rook and drinking Seven-Up. The sound of laughter wells up and bursts through the door and out onto the porch where we lay—hilarity too big for the room to contain.

And always the sound of my mother's shrieks dipping and weaving among the strains of her best friend Esther's giggles. Mom's laughter—it is a melody that underscores my fondest memories.

I decided in those first days of acknowledging the reality of my mother's illness that I would not want for days of tears, and so I would store up the laughter whenever I could. And now, sitting beside her in the darkness, as images of Lucy and Ethel flash before us, I feel it rise from somewhere deep inside of me, a gut-wrenching belly laugh that I fear will wake my father. Mom turns to face me, for a moment surprised, then joining in. Her expression tells me that she's not sure why, but she has never been stingy with joy.

We laugh together about Lucy, Ethel, Esther, childhood, old age, and getting organized. The tears flow with the laughter as we hold hands together in the dark, and mourning holds hands with us, too. But it is good.

There is a time for everything, even in suffering. A time to laugh and a time to weep. A time to gather up the laughter to nourish the heart for the days of mourning. I have found many occasions for laughter in my journey as a caregiver. Those moments nourish my spirit and help me remind myself that God has given me permission to laugh, and He even laughs with me.

Father, You know that sometimes I feel guilty for feeling joy and happiness because of the painful circumstances of my loved one. Please help me to recognize false guilt and to know that even in suffering, we can share times of laughter. Help me to see it as a gift of restoration for a weary heart and a statement of hope in the face of despair.

DESCRIBE A TIME WHEN you laughed with your loved one—it may be a memory from your distant past or something that happened recently. What humor and joy have you found in your caregiving?

_____

_____

_____

_____

_____

_____

_____

_____

_____

_____

_____

Blessed are you who weep now,
for you will laugh.

LUKE 6:21

$\mathcal{I}$ cry a lot these days. I used to apologize for it, but I stopped when I realized tears are a gift. They are a reminder of what is precious now, of what I treasure from the past, and of the promises I hold for the future. My tears are sometimes for what was, sometimes for what is, sometimes for what is to come.

It is Sunday morning, and I stand between my husband and my mother near the back of my parents' church auditorium. Dad stands to Mom's left. I have chosen our spot with deliberation, near an exit where Mom and I can escape with the least disturbance should she grow restless.

Dan grasps my right hand firmly as we stand for worship. A damp tissue nestles between our fingers. It bears my tears today. I cannot seem to worship with my parents beside me without weeping.

My left hand grips Mom's lightly, and I know that she holds Dad's hand on the other side. For most of the worship she has been silent, gazing at the carpet or smiling at a small child across the aisle. Then, at the strains of "Amazing Grace," she quietly lifts her voice in a tremulous alto, and I am lost in tears. I wonder if she has twenty Sundays left to sing beside me . . . ten . . . five?

Sometimes my tears are for what is to come. I know too many friends' stories—stories of their parents' struggles with Alzheimer's. Stories of pain that have caused me to wince and turn aside. I do not want to look too far down the road to the next battle, although I know new battles are coming. I have chosen to face my battles one day at a time, with the resources God has given for that day. My tomorrow tears are an acknowledgment of the suffering and pain that will be part of the next step. Sometimes they overtake me as I'm visiting a nursing home with a friend and I see my mother's future swaddled in an afghan, dozing in a wheelchair. Sometimes they come as I hear my friend talk about her mother's assessment for hospice. But when the tomorrow tears come, I know I will cling to the promise that the same grace that sustains me today will sustain me then.

My tears are also for the joy of knowing that I look past

the pain to what lies beyond. The struggle will increase, but our hope lies in the final purposes of God, revealed and completed when He comes again and when we are together with Him in eternity. My mother has a blessed hope. All sorrow will be wiped away. All tears will be dried. She will see her beloved sister and mother again, and my father and brother and I and all our family will be reunited with her one day. She will still have a glorious alto voice, a passion for others, and a love of watermelon.

My tears are also tears of perspective. I do not have a perfect marriage, a perfect family, a perfect life, a perfect caregiving situation. But I am learning that in the struggle, in the heaviness of life, my only hope lies in turning to the God of the universe, not the gods of the world or the gods of my life for answers.

Sneak up on me at any hour of the day or night, and you might find me in tears. They might be tears of joy, or they might be tears of sorrow. They might be tears of praise, or they might be tears of mourning. But they will all be tears offered to God to redeem for His glory, even in the pain.

Dear Father, You know our sorrows and our fears, and You tell us that our tears are precious to You. You know our deepest pain and weep with us, dear Lord. Thank You that You are the God of all comfort who holds the keys to the universe. You will bring purpose from our pain and redeem our sor-

rows, dear God. Give us the faith to look past the pain to the completed work of Jesus Christ that will wipe away all sorrows. May we turn toward You as our sufficiency in our times of pain, knowing that You offer all that we need.

WHAT DOES IT MEAN for you to turn to God and away from the "gods" of your life in your tears?

_____

_____

_____

_____

_____

_____

_____

_____

_____

_____

Lead Me On, Help Me Stand

But God sent me ahead of you
to preserve for you a remnant on earth
and to save your lives by a great deliverance.

GENESIS 45:7

⧼Light filters through the muslin curtains in dusty shafts, and I breathe in stale air as I watch the motes swirl about me. Dead flies and lady bugs lie strewn on the faded rust carpet as though someone has scattered their dead carcasses in an effort to plant them for a fall harvest.

My mind flickers back to an *Animal Planet* special on brown recluse spiders, and I shudder. At least 263 percent of homes in Missouri are infested with brown recluse spiders, I am sure. I am certain that one is stalking me at this moment, perhaps dangling above my head, ready to pounce. I brush my fingers through my hair and pray that Dan hopes to win my affections by volunteering for attic duty.

I glance about me at the simple furnishings of my father-in-law's tiny living room. A plaid Herculon couch. An Early American pine rocker. A television complete with a rotary channel dial. I thumb through a pile of missionary prayer letters atop a vintage stereo console as I hear the sounds of Dan rummaging in the basement below me. He is already hard at work in another haven for spiders. I decide to volunteer for living room clean-up.

Norman won't be returning to his Missouri home again, and we have forty-eight hours to sort through a lifetime of his possessions with Dan's sister Sue and her husband Jeff, who have flown in from New York, and to decide what to take back to Iowa with us, what to throw out, and what to donate. Although the house is tiny, it's a daunting task. What are the rules for categorizing the acquisitions of a loved one's life?

Following a family strategy session, I'm assigned the front office, a room slightly larger than a deck of cards. Dan and Sue decide to take on the attic, with Jeff's assistance. They know I'm a wimp and are too nice to say it out loud.

Makeshift shelves that Norman has built from lumber scraps from other parts of the house line the walls on three sides. He was never one to use a new nail if an old one could be bent straight. I set to work on the file cabinets. Two hours later I have filled two garbage bags with paperwork and old files that date back to Dan's junior high years.

The next day and a half are spent culling treasures from trash. The Salman's *Head of Christ* that hung over Norman's bed is wrapped in a blanket and tucked safely in a corner of our van. Devotional books are gathered, along with contribution envelopes to dozens of ministries he's supported on the wisp of retirement income that's sustained him for years. Dan discovers his mother's Blue Willow china, his father's navy uniform and World War II rifles, and all are packed in the back of our van, along with a few pieces of furniture and useable items of clothing. The trash is removed, the bed stripped, the house cleaned and left barren in our wake.

When we close the door behind us for the last time, we close a chapter of Norman's life. He will never come back to this house. His strength would not sustain him in the packing, the parting, or the pain. We have shouldered it for him. This stage of his journey is over, and the next has already begun. It has been our job to go ahead of him, to usher him from one world to the next, and to preserve his honor and dignity in the transition.

It was our act of honor to our father to bear him up above the rushing current of transition and turmoil and bear him safely to the other side. We know there will be other journeys, other stages—this will not be the last. We know that in closing one door, we have opened another. But this has not been a task—it has been an act of deliverance and honor for the man we love.

Dear gracious Father, it is difficult to lift those we love up above the rushing current and to bear them to the next place in their journey. But help us to remember that this is a privilege that You have called us to, and You always enable us to fulfill our callings. God, give me the strength to do the difficult tasks that my loved ones can no longer do for themselves. Even when I feel like I must do these things alone, help me to remember that I do them through You and for You.

HAVE YOU HAD TO go ahead of your loved one and prepare the way for them or carry them above the rushing current? How did God enable you in this task?

_____

_____

_____

_____

_____

_____

_____

_____

_____

Every good and perfect gift is from above,
coming down from the Father of the heavenly lights.

JAMES 1:17

$\mathcal{S}$undays in Iowa were a blessing—the blessing of simple memories and laughter and silliness shared with our children while Norman looked on in silence. We were never quite sure what Norman thought of it all. I'd like to believe he enjoyed those times.

When Dan and I moved to Iowa in 2000, we expected to be empty nesters. Recently graduated from college, our daughter Jessica was happily tucked away in Jamaica, working in an orphanage and teaching at a school in a remote bush area. She wasn't sure of her plans beyond Jamaica. She'd always been a moving target, working with the homeless, with battered women, terminally ill children, kids in the projects. We were pretty sure Iowa wouldn't be her first choice when she hit the States again.

We weren't sure at all what our son Nathan had in mind. He was living the life of a prodigal back in Michigan. Nathan had been that child who, by the age of eight, had experienced electrocution through the head, carbon monoxide poisoning, and near drowning. By the age of sixteen, he had been a passenger in a car that had flipped and landed upside down in a swamp, a truck that had plowed through a bedroom and buried itself just shy of the kitchen where Grandma Viva was making apple pies, and in more fender-benders than I want to count.

Then, during Nathan's freshman year in college, we received "The Call Every Parent Dreads." The voice on the other end of the line told us that our son had been an unrestrained passenger in a car that had flipped three times then barrel-rolled twice before landing in oncoming traffic on the other side of the highway. He'd received a closed head injury, an injury that would bring his freshman year to a halt and ripple out into painful consequences for years to come. The day Dan and I left Michigan for Iowa, we knew that we were driving away from a son who was running from God and whom we could not help. We were letting go, and the pain felt like it would rip us in two.

So a few months later, when we received Nathan's call that he wanted to move to Iowa with us, we couldn't express the joy we felt. He said that he wanted to put distance between himself and his former life. It was a first step, and we were ready to meet him there. We cleaned out the basement and met him at the train station.

A few months later Jessica's call came. Her term of service in Jamaica was coming to an end. She needed time to figure out where she was headed next. Maybe she should come home for a time while she sorted it out.

Suddenly the empty nest was full, and we were scrambling for rooms. Dan and I bought Jessica a tiny cabin on a Bible conference grounds near our home for the grand sum of $1,000 and set to work with Nathan gutting and rebuilding it. Nathan moved out of the basement and in with another prodigal whom God was in the process of reclaiming. Together they bound themselves in accountability and sought out a church that embraced ragamuffins. Jessica slid into Nathan's space in the basement while we finished off her cabin, and, all in all, it was two years of Musical Bedrooms as our children came and went.

But in the midst of it all were our Sunday dinners together, times of laughter and giggling while we shared burnt roast and Pillsbury Crescent Rolls. (Did I say that cooking is not one of my gifts?) We simply could not be together without laughing, usually about nothing. Norman would sit silently at the head of the table, and we would cast an occasional question his way. He would raise his head and respond with a monosyllable and, if we were lucky that day, a smile.

Our Sunday dinners were predictable, mundane, and my lifeline to love. They were my children's expression of commitment to Dan and to me and their grandfather. At a time when mental illness had taken so much of the routine from our lives, our dinners together gave it back. They were simple gifts from God, given through the hands of my children. And sometimes the simple gifts are the ones that sustain us most in the difficult times.

Dear Lord, thank You for the people who minister to me in small ways and big ways. Give me a thankful heart, and bless them for their hands of service in my life. Help me to see that there are people around me even now who I can bless through a kind word, a listening heart. Give me the heart of Jesus for those around me and help me see them through His eyes.

HOW CAN YOU come alongside those around you in small ways—through acts of prayer and encouragement? Who has God placed in your path or laid on your heart in this way?

Love must be sincere.
Hate what is evil; cling to what is good.
Be devoted to one another in brotherly love.
Honor one another above yourselves.

ROMANS 12:9–10

We were gathered around the kitchen table for Sunday dinner—Dan, Nathan, Norman, and I. Jessica had driven to Oklahoma to visit a friend for the weekend, so we had abandoned the dining room and packed ourselves around our kitchen table. We were enjoying our usual roast beef, mashed potatoes, crescent rolls, and corn (the only vegetable Nathan would eat), followed by apple pie (Norman's favorite). Since I had only seven meals in my repertoire, Sunday dinners were always a repeat performance, but the kids didn't mind. They knew that any new culinary foray on my part meant something burnt or unrecognizable, so they ate roast with gratitude, week after week.

The call came as I was slicing the pie. I remember distinctly because I was the one who answered the phone, listened briefly, clicked the cordless to *Off*, and made the decision to simply inhale, make the announcement, then collapse and let someone look for the smelling salts.

"That was Jessica. She's on her way back from Oklahoma and wanted everyone to have a chance to adjust to a little piece of news before she got here. She's pierced her nose. I understand it's a lovely little rhinestone in the left nostril."

Norman had always been a man of few words. So few, in fact, that you could throw an entire month's worth into a thimble and still see bottom. My eyes were glued on him in this moment as I struggled with hyperventilation. I thought that if ever a piece of information might prompt Norman to speak, this might be it. His granddaughter who had just returned from the mission field had just pierced her nose. Surely this would be worth at least an "Oh dear."

But not a word. His head, which had been lowered as he stared at his plate in his usual dinnertime posture, reared back, and for a moment I saw his eyes widen. But he never spoke a word. And he never asked *Why?*—then or ever—of me, Dan, or Jessica.

Even Dan and I sometimes felt the awkwardness of our inter-generational living arrangement. Despite the fact that we were fifty and Norman shared our home, we never told him we were going to a movie on the nights when we would slip out to escape into the adventure of someone else's story. Movies had been forbidden in our childhood, and Norman had never darkened the door of a theater, to our knowledge. Our silence was not an act of deceit on our part on our occasional movie nights, but a decision born of respect and protection for a man whose heart and mind were fragile. In many ways we sheltered Dad Beach like a child from things that might grieve his tender heart.

It is never easy to bring adult children back into your home. It is even more difficult to live in harmony as three generations, with a parent who has transitioned into a dependent relationship with children and grandchildren responsible for care and decision making. The key to healthy living as an intergenerational family lies in the concept of honor: of deferring to the spirit and passions of our family members and being devoted to stirring up, with wisdom and respect, the good and the true that God has planted within them. This is not easy because it means preferring others before ourselves—living lives of service for the glory of God alone.

As Jessica drove those few remaining hours from Oklahoma, I prayed for grace to look into her eyes when I met her at the door and to see beyond a glistening piece of glass. I prayed that God would stir up my passion to honor her singular spirit with the same devotion that I honored my father-in-law. I prayed for a spirit that would not condescend and that would embrace her with the acceptance that Christ shows all His children. It was a tough assignment for a mother who was almost fifty. But, thank God, I have a heart still willing to learn.

Dear Father, it is difficult to have generations with different values and different perspectives under one roof. Yet You intended for us to be a gift to each other, to temper one another, to bring balance and perspective, to teach lessons that no one else can teach. Help us to be open to those lessons. Forgive us for our prideful spirits that often blind us to other opinions and other ways of looking at things. Give us hearts of true devotion to one another, born out of sincere love.

WHAT LIFE LESSONS have you learned from generations before you or behind you? In what positive ways do these generations "stretch" your thinking? How can you pray more effectively for the generations within your household?

_____

_____

_____

_____

_____

_____

Being confident of this,
that he who began a good work in you
will carry it on to completion until the day of Christ Jesus.

PHILIPPIANS 1:6

$\mathcal{S}$ome children walk a straight line down the road of life. Others weave from side to side, slamming into Dumpsters and crashing into guardrails. Our son Nathan was a crash-er with a capital C. He was a child who would climb to the roof, jump off and break his leg, then head up to do it again, all with a disarming smile. As he grew older, the smile remained, but the leaps began to take their toll on my heart. During his teen years, I hated to answer the phone when he was out of the house. I was certain that the voice on the other end would be another ER doc, police officer, or irate parent.

When Nathan left for college, Dan and I prayed his education would include courses in Growing Up, both practically and spiritually. We didn't realize that's exactly what God had in mind, except the curriculum wasn't at all what we'd envisioned.

A shot-put, hammer, and discus athlete, Nathan was barely into his freshman semester when a terrible car accident left him with a closed head injury. He'd always struggled with organization and cause-and-effect thinking, but now he couldn't remember if he'd eaten or gone to class, much less done his homework.

Over the next few years, Nathan struggled as we stood by and watched him flounder. Our efforts to get him help were met with passive resistance. His life slipped into a cycle of poor decisions, sinful choices, and spiritual coldness. He dropped out of college and moved out of our home and into an apartment with friends who shared his lifestyle. And when we had to move to Iowa without him, I thought my heart would break.

Three months after we moved, Nathan called and told us he wanted to come home because he wanted to change his life. That was all Dan and I needed to hear. Nathan moved into the basement and immediately found a job in construction. He soon found out he could outwork men with twice his experience, and he dove into his job with fervor. He joined Bible studies and college groups and chose to surround himself with friends and accountability partners.

Dan and I were giddy. Our son was safe in our home and growing in God. Nothing could have delighted us more. So we weren't prepared for the conversation in our sitting room less than a year after he'd moved back in.

"Mom and Dad, I've decided I'm going to move in with my friend Joe and a bunch of us guys who've all been stupid and made the same mistakes. We've decided to live together and be accountable to one another and pursue God together."

My heart sank. This was not my idea of a Spiritual Growth Plan. In fact, it seemed like a recipe for disaster, and I felt panic grip my heart. Nathan was twenty-one, and the ultimate decision would be his. But I was sure he wasn't ready to be on his own yet. It was too soon. Despite our pleas, a month later our son joined the young men in the House of Boys Who'd Blown It, and I hit my knees.

For the first months it was touch and go as Dan and I watched these young men fall down and pull one another to their feet again. Then, gradually, fruit began to blossom as they battled for one another's souls. They learned to confront, to repent, to forgive one another and themselves, and to forgive those who seemed unable to forgive them.

Today these men are living out their faith and are committed to their churches. Our son Nathan is still working in construction, leading Bible studies, and serving in small group ministry in his church.

Sometimes our most loving decision is the decision to step aside and let the battle rage in the lives of those we love, to let them face their struggles and face the God who is sufficient. It is only when they face Him that they can come to know Him.

Dear God, give me faith to step aside and let You work, especially in those times when I desire to influence, to persuade, to make my opinion known. Help me to be silent, trusting Your Holy Spirit to be at work in the hearts of those I love. Thank You for never giving up on prodigals, for loving them even more than we as mothers or fathers or brothers or sisters can love them.

HAVE YOU HAD to step aside and trust the Spirit of God to work in the life of a loved one? How has God reassured you and made His presence known in these times?

_____

_____

_____

_____

_____

_____

_____

_____

*God is faithful; he will not let you be tempted
beyond what you can bear.
But when you are tempted, he will also provide a way out
so that you can stand up under it.
Therefore, my dear friends, flee from idolatry.*

1 CORINTHIANS. 10:13–14

I'm sitting in Dan's tool room among the needle nose pliers and coping saws. It is the farthest place I can run away to and still be in my own house.

I am waiting for Dan to come and find me. That is his role in this psycho-drama, whether he knows it or not. I seethe at the thought that he might still be in bed snoring, oblivious to my suffering here below in the cinderblock bowels of our house.

After all, aren't I the one shouldering most of the sacrifice in caring for his father? Aren't I the one who takes Norman to six different specialists? Aren't I the one fighting to get his pills and his breakfast down him every morning before leaving for school? Aren't I the one juggling a part-time job at school and full-time caregiving at home? Aren't I the one who can't have friends over to the house because of his father's social anxieties? Aren't I . . .

I have my martyr routine down pat. I feel used and abused, and I've invested my bitterness and am reaping long-term dividends. I've learned to manipulate, pout, and lay on guilt so thick I have practically become a Jewish mother.

What I didn't realize that night as I sat staring at a cold wall was that I was a mess because I was waiting for Dan to save me. It was his job to come through for me and bail me out when life got tough. I was sure those words had to have been written into our marriage vows somewhere.

What I learned slowly over the next few years was that I'd developed a mindset of turning to people and things instead of God when life got tough. And whenever our sufficiency is in anyone or anything other than Almighty God, we are guilty of idolatry.

In our Western culture, idolatry isn't usually about statues or pagan worship. It's about substituting other things for God. Every time we're tempted to demand that others come through for us instead of acknowledging that our all-sufficient God provides all that we need and ever will need, we are guilty of idolatry.

That night I fled to the tool room was one of many nights I struggled with self-pity because of a sinful attitude toward my circumstances. The truth was, I was tired, and I was angry. Caring for Norman was difficult, and sometimes I had to do it alone. I did shoulder most of the responsibility for Norman's care, but I was not entitled to anger, bitterness, manipulation, or self-pity.

I was entitled to tell the truth, but balancing truth without bitterness or martyrdom can be difficult for the caregiver. And often we do just need to speak plain, honest truth.

Caregiving is hard, and sometimes I am tired. That doesn't make me a spiritual failure.

Sometimes I need help, and sometimes I need a break, and it's okay to ask. I need breaks to refresh my marriage and my relationships with my children.

Sometimes I need to cry, and sometimes I need a friend's shoulder to do it on.

God is, indeed, faithful. He does not give us more than we can bear. And when we pull our idols from their pedestals and claim His sufficiency in all things, we can begin to see Him truly work.

Dear gracious Father, You know how often I have turned to people and things instead of to You in my difficulties and problems. You know how prone I am to look for solutions everywhere else. My faith is so small, Father. Forgive me for my idolatry. Dear God, give me the faith to turn to You in my need and to throw myself upon Your mercy. Pour out Your grace upon my life. You see my selfishness and bitterness, my manipulation and greed. Forgive me for those sins, Father, and show me how to walk in Your truth and claim Your sufficiency in all things.

WHAT IDOLS HAVE you struggled with or are you currently struggling with? Why are you tempted to turn to these people or things? What do you think God is saying to you about His sufficiency in all things?

_____

_____

_____

_____

_____

_____

_____

_____

_____

_____

*Love the Lord your God with all your heart
and with all your soul and with all your strength . . .
Tie [these commandments] as symbols on your hands
and bind them on your foreheads.*

<small>DEUTERONOMY 6:5, 8</small>

I never realized I was claustrophobic until the first time I was tied up in my hospital bedsheet, my head was clamped into a cage, a towel was draped over my eyes, and I was stuffed into an MRI tube. It was 1999—the year I lost my ability to stand, to walk, to see, to keep my eyes open for more than three minutes without barfing on anything within three feet. It was the year I was diagnosed with a brain lesion the size of a walnut nestled near my brain stem.

I was in Europe helping conduct a travel-study tour when the earliest symptoms hit—waves of fatigue, loss of balance, then a crushing headache. Back in the States days later, I lay in the neuro-oncology unit of Detroit Medical Center in a fetal position with my eyes closed, vomiting and praying. Of all the places I had envisioned being the center of attention, a neuro-oncology unit had never ranked among my top contenders. Every day my symptoms worsened as doctors searched for the cause of the blob in my brain. Stroke? MS? Viral inflammation? (A myriad of symptoms and a bazillion dollars later, I still have no answers.)

Seven years out from that time in my life, I have learned many things. I have learned to walk again (in my own rather erratic way), thanks, in part, to massive doses of steroids that shrunk my lesion. I have also learned that life with neurological damage can be an adventure and that I would fit better in an MRI tube if they'd just slather me up with a bit of Pam cooking spray before sliding me in.

But most of all, I have learned that God gives grace in the airless, tight spaces of life. We often hear Him most clearly when we are trussed up like a chicken with our heads clamped down and our eyes shrouded from the world. I know I did.

The question that echoed through my mind during that first MRI scan in 1999 has echoed through my mind in the years since: *If these really are your final days, what do you regret, what do you wish you had done differently?*

Seven years out from my first MRI, the question still

resonates in my heart as I care for my father-in-law in his final days on earth. It shadows my thoughts as I care for my mother who is succumbing to the ravages of Alzheimer's, and it pulls at the corners of my soul as I watch my father rake in a few raggedy breaths as he walks to the mailbox.

Someday I will look back on these days, and I know that my measuring stick for regret cannot be that I tried to do everything and to be everything to everyone I loved who had a need. God asks that I bring a measuring stick of integrity to my life—to each day and each task—knowing that I can trust Him for what I cannot do and what I cannot see. I can trust Him in the small, tight spaces, when I am trussed up like a chicken in the dark, with the sides pressing in and I can do nothing. I can trust Him to give me the ability to be still and lie quietly while He works. I can trust Him to do exceedingly abundantly beyond what I can do myself. I cannot meet every need. I cannot take away every pain. I cannot fend off the inevitability of a difficult death. But I can love my loved one and rest in the truth that God has provided and is providing all things for them that I cannot.

These days my constant companions are three-by-five cards with specially selected verses of Scripture written out. They are stuffed in my purse, stuck in my pockets, stuck to my steering wheel. Sometimes they come through the laundry faded and tattered at precisely the right moment. And they remind me that a life lived in integrity and love will be a life that knows no regret.

Father, You know the tight spaces of my life today, and You know that I can't do everything that looks like it needs to be done. You know the claustrophobic places of my heart and that I want to crawl out of this place in my life. But You have placed me here, and You will supply every good thing that I need for each and every moment of each and every day. Help me to live this day with integrity, striving to honor You in what I do and trusting You to fill in all the blank spaces that I cannot fill. Most of all, may I grow each day in loving You with all my heart, soul, and mind as I learn to trust You.

WHAT ARE SOME OF THE "tight spaces" of your life right now? What does it mean for you to walk in integrity and honor God in what you do today?

_____

_____

_____

_____

_____

_____

_____

_____

A friend loves at all times,
and a brother is born for adversity.

PROVERBS 17:17

ears are the glue of the soul. When you weep with a friend, you bind your heart to theirs.

Cindy's soul and mine are stuck together in one messy lump of tears and wadded tissues, with a few candy wrappers thrown in for good measure. Our hearts melted together one Christmas morning when she trusted me enough to let me crawl into a hospital bed with her critically ill preemie so she could go home and celebrate the holiday with her two other small children and her husband.

I'd come to know Cindy Alwood through my daughter Jessica, who babysat her two older children during her pregnancy for her triplets. Then the first triplet died in utero, and the other two came prematurely. Stacy lived only a few weeks, and Alicia, the only surviving triplet, was struggling for her life when Jessica returned to college in the fall. News of Cindy and Alicia came to me through our church and Christian school throughout the winter, but I really only knew Cindy from a distance.

When Jessica came home that Christmas, we learned that Cindy was once again in the hospital with Alicia. Everyone who knew the Alwoods knew that Cindy never left Alicia's side and that the family would be separated for their first Christmas. The thought tore at me. Adam and Stephanie, just three and five, would be without their mother on Christmas morning.

The thought of helping out didn't seem like a big decision at the time. My kids were both in college, and Christmas morning had lost its magic for them. They'd just as soon open gifts on Christmas Eve, sleep in on Christmas Day, and get up late for a mid-morning brunch. If I could talk Cindy into trusting me for a few hours with her baby, everybody would win. She knew and trusted Jessica. I figured it was worth a try.

Maybe it was my personal charm. Maybe it was the fact that Jessica and I could offer a two-on-one caregiver-to-baby ratio. Or maybe it was the fact that Cindy was desperate to spend the morning with her family. But the answer was *Yes*, and Jessica and I took turns crawling into the oxygen tent and holding the tiny girl who would grab onto our hearts and never let go. It was my first hospital visit with Cindy and Alicia. I still have not seen my last.

By the age of eight, Alicia had undergone forty-two brain surgeries. She was struggling through a failed shunt revision in 1999 and was in Detroit Children's Hospital when I became deathly ill with my brain lesion a building away at Detroit Medical Center's Harper Hospital. The buildings are connected by an underground system of tunnels, and on my sickest day, Alicia was wheeled to my room through the underground tunnels and was placed in my bed. The two of us lay together, heads reeling, eyes twitching, stomachs wretching, but one in spirit. She was released before I was on that visit, but she called to check on me every day. She is my "brain buddy," and for years we have shared the same headaches on the same days, even when we've been separated by time zones.

Ten years and two moves later, Cindy and I remain glued. She has struggled through the pain of loss, of watching her child disintegrate beneath the attacks of disease. She has mourned the death of two children and has faced her own terminal diagnosis and recovery. She has battled the strains of caregiving on her marriage, on her children, on her health, on her hope. She knows pain and she knows tears, and she has been an unfailing friend to me in my pain and suffering.

Tears are the glue of the soul. When you weep with

a friend, you bind your heart to theirs, and both of your souls are strengthened.

Dear gracious God, thank You for the friends You have placed in my life who have been there to catch my tears. Make me the kind of friend to others who can listen, can affirm, can love. Make me an instrument of Your peace and Your healing in the lives of others. Give me a gentle touch, a listening heart, an ear quick to listen and a tongue slow to speak.

WHO HAS BLESSED your life by weeping with you? How has this ministered to your heart?

_____

_____

_____

_____

_____

_____

_____

_____

_____

_____

Sing praises to the Lord,
enthroned in Zion . . .
he does not ignore the cry of the afflicted.

PSALM 9:11, 12

$\mathcal{I}$ was fourteen years old the first time I swore in my mother's presence. I'd slammed the door of our 1969 Impala station wagon as a statement of protest against her staunch refusal to allow me to go to a school dance. In that moment of frustration, my fingers, clenched tightly in anger, did not release their grip and became suddenly, inextricably wedged between the car door and the door frame.

The word that flew from my lips stopped my mother dead in her tracks. If I had not been pinned in place by a two-ton vehicle, I would have fled for my life. I will never forget the shame I felt that day, believing that some vile place in my heart had just been exposed before my mother and that I had irreparably grieved her.

My mother was eighty the first time I heard her swear. I, too, stopped dead in my tracks. It was on one of those days when we were first realizing that bras and panties had become enigmas beyond her comprehension. I had placed her clothes beside her on the bed that morning and sat in a chair opposite, waiting for her to slip into the garments one by one. But she seemed mystified and grew agitated as I began to help, slapping away my hands and finally letting fly with an earthy expletive. Instantly, a sense of shame washed over me, as though in that moment in time I had become a voyeur peering through a window into a dark recess of my mother's heart, a place I did not know existed.

Words often spoken to me by well-intentioned friends rolled through my mind, words that had often seemed trite. "Remember, it's not your mother, Shelly, it's the disease."

And they are right. Alzheimer's, like other dementias, is an affliction, a great suffering. And God has made clear His regard for the heart cries of the afflicted: those who are troubled, agitated, grieved, distressed, under continued pain or persecution. He listens. This is what separates my teenage words from the cries torn from the lips of my mother. Her cursings come from a place of torment and suffering known to Jesus Christ Himself. Her cries of *Oh, God* are not a violation of the Third Commandment but a prayer that falls upon the heart of a loving, compassionate Father with outstretched arms.

Jesus came for the diseased and the afflicted, the broken down and beaten up. He came for the rumpled and unlovely, the coarse and the wicked. He sees the words that fly from our hearts and lips and those that do not, and He loves us in spite of it all. Our sin does not render Him speechless or powerless. Instead, it impelled Him to make eternal sacrifice on our behalf and to love us in spite of our unloveliness. It's a love that leaves us breathless in the knowledge of our own afflictions.

Unconditional love.

Unequivocal love.

Immeasurable, eternal love poured out on our unloveliness.

Sing praises to the Lord.

Father, You know how hard it is for me to hear my loved one speak in unlovely ways. Comfort me with the truth that You are a God who hears the cries of the afflicted. You know the anguish of my loved one's mind and body. Help me to rest in the truth that their heart cries are precious to You. Honor them and bless this dear one of mine, Father. Thank You for unconditional, unequivocal, immeasurable love that sees past all of our unloveliness.

HOW HAVE YOU struggled with seeing "affliction" in the mind and body of your loved one? What specific heart cries would you like to share with God on their behalf?

*Not that people will see that we have stood the test
but that you will do what is right even though
we may seem to have failed.
For we cannot do anything against the truth,
but only for the truth.*

2 CORINTHIANS 13:7–8

$\mathcal{I}$ stood in the bathroom of my parents' home at 2:00 A.M., my father crumpled and moaning at my feet as blood gushed from his head and my mother wandered, unclothed, in the hallway, calling for her husband. She apparently did not want to claim the rather messy one lying prostrate on the bathroom floor. It was Day Two of my four-day visit. I was there with the specific objective of helping Mom get launched on the road to recovery from a bout of double pneumonia. And since Day One had been about as much fun as a root canal without anesthetic, at this point in time I began to think that perhaps my plan was going south.

Who would have thought that my simple desire to take care of my parents for a few days could turn into an episode of *Rescue 9-1-1*, with blood and guts and police (well, sort of), and ambulances and multiple hospitals and a rescue run all the way from Iowa to Michigan and back?

It began over the Christmas holidays near Detroit at Paul and Sheryl's (my brother and sister-in-law) in the midst of general family mayhem and gifts and gluttony when Mom showed signs of coming down with a bug of some sort. I agreed to drive home to Muskegon, on the west side of the state, with my parents and get Mom in for a doctor's appointment within the next few days while Dan returned to Iowa. I could take the train back home at the end of the week, and that would be that. But by the time Mom, Dad, and I reached Muskegon, it was apparent Mom was too sick to wait. I had only one choice: take her to the emergency room in the late afternoon on New Year's Eve.

The room was crowded with parents holding sick and crying children. Every seat was taken, and a teenager who was clutching his stomach stood and politely (and heroically) gave his seat to my mother. I explained our situation to a rather beleaguered-looking triage nurse who could not have been more apologetic. Unfortunately, a number of critical cases had come in just before we'd arrived. Our only choice was to wait, as Mom's whimpers escalated.

It was three hours before Mom was seen. Five hours before she was x-rayed. Six hours before we were told Mom had double pneumonia. Seven hours before we were released. But we had survived. I knew Day Two could only get better.

Now, standing in the bloodstained bathroom where my father had fallen and cracked his head against the bathtub, I didn't know what to do first. Stanch the bleeding? Call 9-1-1? Throw an afghan over my mother so as not to startle the paramedics when they arrived?

I decided to multi-task and doused a washcloth in water and tossed it in my father's direction while I grabbed the phone. I had barely managed to slide a robe over my mother's shoulders before Joe, my parents' neighbor and an assistant prosecuting attorney for the county, was through the door packing heat. My parents barely sneezed without Joe arriving on the scene with a tissue. Thank God for Joe, who stayed with my mom while I rode to the hospital with my father to get his head put back together.

By the next morning we were home again, but it was my turn to collapse as a flu bug overcame me. Mom was lying feverish and listless in one room, Dad was wandering the house with a glazed look, and I was unable to lift my head. There was no way I could get on a train and ride to Iowa. I called Dan for the hundredth time in seventy-two hours and begged him to come and get me. Sheryl would come and stay with my parents and help oversee their care while Dan drove seven hours from Iowa to claim the remains of his wife.

Although it seemed that everything I did over those few days failed, in the eyes of God, nothing failed. When our goal is love, our goal can never be blocked. In spite of blood and general mayhem and tasks unmet, I doled out abundant love on that trip.

Caregiving is never measured by tasks and always by love.

> *Father, what freedom there is in knowing that our true goals of ministering Your love in truth and grace can never be blocked. We cannot fail when our goal is to pour out Your love in the lives of others. Help me to see that although I often stand amid chaos, I am not a failure in Your eyes. Help me to see that as long as I stand and act in accordance with Your truth, nothing can stand against me.*

WHEN ARE YOU TEMPTED to feel like a failure? What does it mean to stand in God's truth at these times in your life?

_____

_____

_____

_____

_____

_____

_____

You were wearied by all your ways,
but you would not say, "It is hopeless."
You found renewal of your strength,
and so you did not faint.

ISAIAH 57:10

I am sitting in my driveway, and I am waiting.

I've spent the day going head-to-head with teenagers on the usual issues: food fights, dress code for the senior trip, implications of sliding down the school banister from a height of twenty-eight feet, reasons why you shouldn't move into your best friend's home at the age of fifteen without your parents' permission, to name a few.

So when I go home, I want to do one of two things: hide or unleash—in, of course, the most appropriate of ways. I want to devour an entire box of Oreos or watch *Judge Judy* and tell myself that my students are lucky I'm not more like her. I want to turn on *Sweatin' to the Oldies* and put on my hospital scrubs and scream the lyrics with Richard Simmons. But I can't do either. I'm "on duty" the moment I cross the threshold.

My driveway moments are moments when I gather myself for the next task, when I renew myself for the role that meets me on the other side of the door.

There's a long list of "I can'ts" that settle over me when I enter the door of my house. Like the long list of things Dan and I can't openly talk about anymore—things that are personal or distressing. Because I'm responsible for counseling high school girls, I'm responsible for working with young women who are suicidal, anorexic, bulimic, cutters, who've been or know someone who's been sexually or physically abused. And because Dan is my high school principal, these matters often require that we spend long hours in discussion.

Work discussions and family discussions now have to take place behind closed doors. Norman's health and Norman's honor have required that we establish a new standard of conduct in our home. Our caregiver roles now supersede many of our personal rights, and Dan and I have had to find ways to deal with that tension.

Looking back over seven years of caregiving, I've come to recognize that the most important space that Dan and I have carved out for ourselves has been on the back of our Harley-Davidson motorcycle. Avid bikers, we've been riding since before we were married. In fact, our second date was on a motorcycle, and it was Dan's Yamaha 650 that helped him win my heart.

The secret to our biking is that, apart from the crazy friends Dan and I ride with, we're absolutely alone together when we ride. Riding is a place for us. It takes us to the center of God's creation, with the wind slapping us in the face and the vibrations of the road beneath us chattering our bones. (If you're a biker, you get it, and if you're not a biker, you don't.) My heart has sung more verses of the doxology on the back of our motorcycle than my lips have ever sung within the sanctuary of a church. In the rawness of the wind and the rain and the sunshine, I am reminded that the God of the Universe is indescribable beyond comprehension, magnificent beyond anything we can envision.

Not everyone will find that place in their soul on the back of a Harley. But I challenge you to find a place that refreshes you, that fills you, that feeds you, that reminds you of the nearness of the amazing God who holds you in the palm of His hand. That place may be in a tent in a campground. It may be at a retreat. It may be gazing on the beauty of a Renoir or a Monet at an art museum. It may be floating on the waves of your favorite pond or mushing behind a dogsled. It may be in a week of solitude with your Bible and a notebook in the family cabin.

Caregiving is wearying. Often our homes are not places of rest. Find your own "Harley" and hunker down to find refreshment for your soul so that you do not grow faint in the battle.

Dear Lord, so often we battle against weariness of spirit, as well as weariness of body and mind. Help me to be committed to the task of carving out spaces of refreshment for my body, emotions, and spirit. Direct me to places where I can do this with my family, Lord, where we can find pockets of restoration and refreshment together. Father, I ask that You direct us specifically to a place of rest over these next months.

WHAT ARE YOUR "Harley" places of refreshment? Who needs to be refreshed along with you? How can you work toward planning respite for yourself in the months ahead? What resources are available to you in your planning?

_____

_____

_____

_____

_____

_____

_____

_____

I Am Tired, I Am Weak, I Am Worn

Be at rest once more, O my soul,
for the Lord has been good to you.
For you, O Lord, have delivered my soul from death,
my eyes from tears, my feet from stumbling,
that I may walk before the Lord in the land of the living.

PSALM 116:7–9

Christians aren't supposed to be mentally ill. And certainly not missionaries.

Nobody ever really spoke those words out loud to Dan or to me. But we saw *the look* flash over people's faces hundreds of times when we told them about Norman, Dan's father, a retired missionary who walked so closely with God that he spoke in the plural *we* when he spoke of the details of his routine, with the intimacy of one who'd spent the day with a friend.

Ah, a saint of God, a hero, their eyes would say. They'd smile and nod as we would explain the need for moving

Norman into our home to care for him. Then, with the words *mental illness,* their smiles would slowly give way to looks of confusion.

Mentally ill missionary. It was an oxymoron, right?

To be honest, when I told people about Norman's mental illness, I felt defensive, at least in the early days. Your liver enzymes are allowed to go on holiday to the south of France, and you can still be considered spiritual if your kidneys fail. But let your brain cells get a little feisty, or the chemicals above your neck get out of whack, and a lot of people are willing to smack labels on you faster than a butcher in a meat market.

There were plenty of other physical illnesses I could have chosen to concentrate on when I talked about Norman—his bad heart, his strokes, his broken hip that had never healed properly, his cancer, his struggles with malnutrition. But his mental illness was his most painful struggle and ours. It was the struggle that brought him into our home. It was the struggle that tore at the fiber of our family for the five-and-a-half years we cared for him. It was our deepest pain and our constant companion. It overshadowed every moment of our lives as his caregivers, and it was a thorn in his flesh that God did not choose to fully remove.

When we began our journey with Norman, Dan and I feared that mental illness would cast a cloud of indignity over the most dignified and honorable man we had ever known. We felt embarrassed about something many churches were unwilling to speak about, teach about, and help families deal with.

What I learned over the next years, however, was that no one could take Norman's dignity from him. He did not lose it the first day I helped him dress. He did not lose it the day he was admitted into the psychiatric unit or regain it the day he was released. He did not lose it because of the drugs he took or the diagnoses he received. No illness or disease could take it from him. It was not a reflection of his appearance, his behavior, or other people's attitudes. His dignity, like his identity, was secure in Christ.

The moment I began to accept that truth, my attitude began to change. The shame I had felt slipped away. I discussed Norman's illnesses freely and openly, both the challenges and the encouragement that we saw in his treatment. I sought out others who could benefit from the resources that had been so helpful to us. I discovered that there were dozens of people in our Christian community who had family members who struggled with mental illness, as well, and felt they had nowhere to turn for spiritual support.

I found rest in the knowledge that even Norman's mental illness had passed through God's hands. Over the next five-and-a-half years, we would find abundant reasons to praise God in the midst of Norman's mental illness and abundant reasons for tears. But in all things, we praised God for the precious life of a saint, a man of dignity, who will always be our hero.

Father, You alone know how hard it is to see my loved one suffer the ravages of mental illness. Give me eyes to see them as You see them, beyond the disease. Restore my faith in a future and a hope for my loved one, for it is so easy for me to believe that there is no purpose in this suffering. I claim the truth that You are walking before us in this. Give me a heart to praise You for the blessings and a heart to trust You.

HAVE YOU HAD to struggle with people's perceptions of mental illness, physical illness, or suffering? How have you dealt with those perceptions? What has God taught you through those times?

_____

_____

_____

_____

_____

_____

_____

_____

*N*orman and I are playing a game. I am spooning pills into his mouth, and he is spitting them back at me. The score is ten-zip in his favor.

The kitchen clock reads 10:30. I am due at work at 10:00. I feel the knots gripping my stomach, and I swallow the sobs that I feel rising in my throat. They will come later, when I get to school and allow myself the luxury of falling apart in the privacy of Dan's office.

Yesterday we played the sitting game. I'd coaxed Norman from his bedroom and into the kitchen where his breakfast waited, laid out in a precise arrangement on a placemat. A bowl of oatmeal. Always a bowl of oatmeal. A peeled and sectioned orange. Apple juice. But despite my cajoling, pleading, urging, gentle pressure, and even tugging, Norman refused to sit. He'd clenched the chairback in a death grip as he'd stared straight ahead, silent and unblinking.

I was late for work that morning, too. Morning after morning, I'd struggled to get Norman out of bed, to get him dressed, to get him to take his medications, to eat before his health aide came to the house so I could leave for school. With each passing day, he'd receded more and more into some dark corner of his mind where we could not reach him. And with each passing day, his thin frame had become more emaciated.

As the days passed, Dan and I struggled to know what doctor to try next. We'd already been to Mayo Clinic, and the medications they'd prescribed hadn't eased Norman's symptoms at all. In fact, they were increasing.

Then one afternoon our son Nathan called. He'd been staying with us and helping us care for Grandpa, and he was panicked.

"Mom and Dad, you've got to come home. The police and an ambulance are here. Grandpa called 9-1-1 and reported that someone had poisoned me. I've told them that he's confused and they're checking him over, but they need you here now."

The next few days were a blur. More doctors, more evaluations. A nursing home admission while Dan and I drove to Missouri to get papers needed for Norman's personal affairs. And while we were in Missouri, the call that Norman was being asked by the nursing home to temporarily admit himself to a psychiatric unit at our local hospital.

Dan and I were stunned. The guilt of not being able to be with him or help him understand what was happening tore at our hearts. The excruciating hour Dan spent with his dad on the phone that day helping to persuade him to admit himself was the most difficult and loving thing I've ever watched my husband do.

There are times when we must face the truth that our resources are limited. We cannot do it all, and God never intended for us to. In an ocean of need, we have only the cup He has placed in our hands.

There are times when we must do the best thing for our loved one, and that best thing is often the hard thing they cannot do for themselves. And the hardest thing can be admitting that we cannot take away pain, protect our loved one from suffering, or stave off disease or death.

On difficult days we rested in the greater truth that our heavenly Father's resources are not limited. He is sufficient in all things, and that is enough.

Dear Father, You know that I struggle with a compulsion to meet every need, take away every pain, and protect my loved one from every hard thing about their disease and their circumstances. But my resources are limited—my body, my time, my family, my knowledge, my energy. Give me the wisdom to know that I cannot do it all and that You do not expect me to. Grant me the ability to rest when I am surrounded by an ocean of need, knowing I have only a cup in my hand. Help me to rest in the truth that Your resources are unlimited, and that You are sufficient for every need.

HAVE YOU FACED a time in your caregiving where you had to make difficult decisions on behalf of your loved one? How did God sustain you in that time of difficulty?

_____

_____

_____

_____

_____

_____

_____

_____

_____

_____

I have never visited a mental institution before. Scenes from *One Flew Over the Cuckoo's Nest* flicker through my mind as someone on the other side of the metal doors buzzes us through. For reasons too unfamiliar to name, I am embarrassed. I wonder if people who see Dan and me passing through this portal know it is the psychiatric unit of the hospital. I wonder if they feel sorry for us or wonder why we are there.

We walk down a hallway that leads to a nurses' station manned by three middle-aged women discussing a Hollywood celebrity. They smile brightly and I smile back, somewhat less brightly. I am asked to leave my purse. It occurs to me that security risks lurk within its depths. A nail file. My Excedrin. Dan is asked to leave his keys. The implications of this simple request hit me like a slap in the face. This is a place where people protect you from yourself.

No one could ever have prepared us for this—for visiting a parent in a mental facility. I am not sure how to act, much less how to feel. I grip Dan's hand tightly, knowing that it's the one right thing to do. The doctor will be out shortly to discuss Norman's admission with us, we are told. We're directed to wait in the lounge area where patients gather to watch television, read, or talk.

We choose the seats closest to the nurses' station. A young girl who appears to be college age walks a circuit near us, circling a grouping of chairs in the center of the room. She holds a teddy bear in her arms and occasionally whispers something. Her voice is soft, and I cannot hear what she is saying.

Norman's eyes first told us that something was wrong when his words could not. In those first days after he moved into our home, there were few words. Within days, even those slipped away as he retreated somewhere deep within himself.

When we brought Norman back from his tiny home in Missouri and into our home, our desire was to love, protect, and honor him. In our minds, that would "look" like nurturing, caring things. But we never expected nurture and care to look like a hospital psychiatric unit.

At times God's best care, His best plan for us, takes us to places that seem cold, harsh, unwelcoming. At times we go reluctantly because we have never envisioned those places as places of nurture and care. But I thank God for a hospital unit that for six weeks enfolded my father-in-law and provided the care he needed to get well enough to return to our home again. God's presence was not limited to the walls of my home. God's touch was not limited to Dan's hands or my hands.

Dan and I walked through the doorways of that psychiatric unit daily for weeks. And in the years ahead, we would walk through the doors of nursing homes, assisted living centers, rehabilitation centers, and hospitals in our caregiving journey with Norman and with my parents. And God was present in each place with them in the same way He was present with them in our own home. His love and care did not stop at my door. I can rest in the knowledge that it extends beyond my hands but can never extend beyond His.

Dear Lord, I know that I too often rely on what I see and how I feel when I think about Your care for me and my loved ones. But I know that Your care is not limited by walls and buildings and people and circumstances. Help me to rest in the truth that I cannot be anywhere apart from Your presence and Your care. Give me a gracious acceptance of my circum-

stances and the circumstances of my loved one. Help me to see the blessings of provision that You have made for them, even in the small things. Give me a spirit of thanksgiving that allows me to bless the hearts of those around me.

WHAT ASPECTS OF your circumstances can you praise God for? Where has it been hardest for you to "see" God's presence with your loved one? How has God provided for you in that place?

Be completely humble and gentle;
be patient, bearing with one another in love.

Ephesians 4:2

𝒪f you listen closely to the wedding videos of my niece, Keri, you will hear the sounds of someone snorting from somewhere in the second row.

I would like to blame the snorting on someone else, but every family member knows it was me. I am known to cry most unceremoniously at weddings, but I have never been a delicate crier like some women, who can dab their eyes daintily and sniff. I snort and slobber and generally require heaping amounts of tissues. This is one reason I require a large purse.

My crying is somewhat representative of the rest of me. My laughter is generally loud, my cooking burnt. My family is a family of strong, opinionated people, and we are all willing to tell you why we are right. My mother was the exception and let us each think our opinions were the best. She was probably the smartest of us all.

The first time Dan met my parents, he took me out on the back porch and asked me *why* we all spoke to each other the way we did. I didn't know what on earth he was talking about. He seemed to think we were arguing, and I had to explain that we Burkes weren't arguing at all, but that people in my family usually saw things from different perspectives and that everybody thought it was their job to prove to everybody else that their way of looking at things was the best way. That wasn't arguing, was it?

So it has always baffled me that God, in His infinite wisdom, decided to plop Norman Beach, a man you had to do the Heimlich Maneuver on to force an opinion from his body, into the home of a Burke, in the midst of a clan of Burkes.

Norman was a man of long silences. He desired nothing more than solitude and quietness and the opportunity to be alone with God. It was the driving force in his life.

So why did God pick my home to be Norman's home, where chaos reigned and dinner was served at the sound of the smoke alarm (unless it was take-out)? And what about the shock for Norman of living among Burkes, especially during our family holidays, when our idiosyncrasies burst forth on center stage?

I sometimes wondered if God placed Norman with us

so that he, aghast at our Burke-ness, would redouble his prayer efforts on our behalf after our wild Christmas gatherings at Paul and Sheryl's, with rollicking karaoke, hilarious rounds of Catch Phrase, and incessant games of Rook to a symphony of ringing cell phones. Perhaps that was God's purpose.

Or perhaps it was simply so Norman would feel embraced by people who were free with embraces. He was not a demonstrative man, but perhaps God was giving us the opportunity to help him catch up.

Or maybe God put Norman in our family so we would be blessed to see the face of humility, grace, and composure bowed in prayer at our family table. Perhaps it was so we would have the opportunity to study a countenance that emanated contentment and learn from it.

Norman's face and Norman's life showed us what it meant to be still and know God. He knew joy in sitting in the presence of his God, his Bible in his lap, and listening for the Holy Spirit to move in his heart. He was a man comfortable with silences because the silences had taught him to listen.

Norman taught me about stillness and serenity in the midst of chaos. And he embraced my life for eternity by teaching me the beauty of silence. Perhaps that was God's purpose.

Dear Father God, at the very center of my relationship with You is the need for me to be still and listen. Father, I desire to speak to You from the core of my being, understanding that prayer is the true expression of my heart to You. Father, I desire to increase my passion and commitment to spend more time with You in prayer and in stillness before You, listening to You as You share Your heart with me.

CHOOSE A SPECIAL passage of Scripture, perhaps a Psalm or familiar passage, and read it through several times. Then meditate on that passage for a period of time and ask God what He desires to show you from that Scripture. Write down relevant passages and carry them with you throughout the day and continue to ask God to apply the truth of those passages to your heart. Record the things the Spirit of God lays on your heart.

_____

_____

_____

_____

_____

_____

_____

_____

_____

_____

My soul finds rest in God alone;
my salvation comes from him.

PSALM 62:1

$\mathcal{W}$hen I was a child, I loved to run away to the crawl space beneath our house. It was the perfect hiding place— safe, warm, secure. I was perhaps eight or ten in those days when it was high adventure to slip out the back door of the house without permission and disappear beneath the metal storm door, slipping it closed above my head.

I would sit cross-legged on the apron of concrete that fanned out at the mouth of the crawl space entrance for a dozen feet or so, before it dropped off into the soft Michigan sand that lay like a cushion beneath the rest of the house. Above me, I could hear the footfalls of my parents and my brother, even the soft murmurings of their voices. Most often I would sit and wonder if they missed me, if they knew that I was gone, if at any moment they would throw their hands into the air and cry, "Shelly, where *are* you, dear Shelly?" Usually I would sit there until my bottom got cold and the daddy long-legs got too close, and then I would give up and slip back into the house and pretend that I had been in the backyard. It was humiliating to never even have been missed.

In the past few years of my life, I have found other hiding places to run to. My favorite hideaway has been the loft of my daughter Jessica's Iowa cabin, where I lie on a mattress tucked beneath the gentle slope of the roof. Her cabin is a place born from the corporate sweat of our family brows—purchased from a tiny Bible conference for a pittance and gutted to the warped and crooked studs, then rebuilt with our bare hands. It is decorated in soft yellows and bold reds, the colors of my daughter's spirit. It is a place that feeds my soul with rich memories—memories of Jessica and Nathan and Dan and me arguing and laughing, wielding hammers and nail guns and straddling rafters. Memories of Nathan wedged in a hole in the wall like Winnie the Pooh, and Jessica in a bandana working the chop saw. Memories of Dan running wiring for the third time and me bailing spilled paint from freshly finished wood floors with a Dixie Cup and no running water.

The cabin is a place where I go to remind myself that the best things are often not the perfect things, but the things you must work at the most. It's not hard to see the imperfections in the drywall. I mudded the front bedroom myself, and I am button-bustin' proud of my work, even though my friend George the cabinetmaker (and the most gracious perfectionist I have ever known) probably cringes inwardly when he views my work. But what matters is that the cabin was our family labor of love.

The past seven years have taught me that like mudding the front bedroom, I only have to be willing to pick up the trowel and give caregiving my best effort.

God is not standing back judging my efforts with the eye of the perfectionist. He looks at my heart and says it is good. He sees me through the righteousness of His Son, and I do not have to fear imperfection or ineptitude. I am equipped for the task to which He has called me. If I am called to do the wiring three times, it is because it is in His plan, and it is not my concern. I can trust all things to His care.

My rest is not found in a place, it is found in a Person— Jesus Christ.

Dear Father God, thank You for giving me the freedom to be imperfect. Help me to grant myself the freedom that You so graciously extend to me and to know that You only ask that I come to each day with a desire to honor You as I pick up the trowel. Give me the peace that comes through knowing You intimately and being rooted in my relationship with You, for all freedom flows from my relationship with You, dear Father. May I learn more and more each day to find rest in You alone.

WHAT DOES IT MEAN for you to rest in God? How does meditating on Scripture help you rest in truth? What Scriptures are especially meaningful to you?

_____

_____

_____

_____

_____

_____

_____

_____

_____

_____

Surely the Sovereign Lord does nothing
without revealing his plan to his servants the prophets.

AMOS 3:7

I don't know how many times I've wished that God would take up skywriting. I know a lot of my friends feel this way, too. If God would just *show* us, we would *do* it, we say, usually when we're in the middle of a Major Life Decision.

Well, Dan and I were in the middle of a Major Life Decision of the painful variety. After almost thirty years in Christian school administration, our lives had not lacked for these types of decisions, and you would think we would have gotten pretty good at making them. (Just spend more time in devotions and prayer, and God will direct you to a specific verse in Hezekiah with your next address on it.) But this is not the way things usually worked out for Dan and me. And it was not the way things were working out this time.

There were only a few things we were certain of that summer: that we were doing our very best to get back to Michigan and move as close as possible to my parents to help with their care; that Dan only had four paychecks left; and that we still didn't have a clue where we were going. Our networking, calls, and interviews had turned up nothing. The only real possibility that existed was an Iowa head-hunter who was offering Dan the opportunity to move into the corporate world at an exorbitant pay increase, with the caveat that we be willing to move anywhere in the country.

On a Saturday evening as we sat down to discuss our options, I reminded Dan of a Christian school not far from my parents that he'd expressed interest in over the years. Had he called them?

"They've had my resume for years, Shelly, and I called them last year and the year before and they weren't interested. But I'll give it another shot."

I could see the defeat in his eyes as he spoke.

On Monday the phone rang as I was packing boxes in our bedroom for a move I didn't know if we were ever going to make.

"May I speak to Dan, please? This is Barb from Algoma Christian."

I told her that Dan was out at the moment and thanked her for returning his call. I sensed her hesitation before she responded.

"Returning his call? No one here has spoken to Dan. Last night, the superintendent and I were looking over his resume we have on file and we were calling to ask if he'd be interested in interviewing for a position we have open."

I slowly let out my breath.

"That's pretty amazing, Barb, because Dan planned to call you this morning to see if you might have a position open. He's always thought highly of your school. I know he'd love to interview with you."

I thought about adding, "Would sometime tomorrow work for you guys, since we only have four paychecks left?" but thought better of it.

A few weeks later our biker buddies Marcia and Steve were helping us sling boxes into trucks as we packed for Michigan. This time we would leave Norman behind in a nursing home until we could get settled and bring him home with us. This time we'd leave Nathan behind again, but restored to God and enfolded in the arms of a local church. And this time we'd leave Jessica, too, but she was preparing for her next mission trip that would take her to Germany and Indonesia, where she would do tsunami relief work and look to the skies for her own messages from God.

Our four years in Iowa were a womb of healing and protection for our family. It was a place where God showed us that He does reveal His plans in His way, and we just have to be faithful in the waiting.

Dear Lord, there is often nothing more difficult than waiting when we cannot see what is ahead. But it is Your mercy that does not allow us to see the next step, for it is in the waiting and the watching that our faith grows. Forgive us for our demanding spirit in wanting to see You at work, Father. Increase our faith to trust that You are always at work—behind us, around us, within us, before us.

WHEN HAVE YOU wanted God to "skywrite" in your life? How did He choose to work instead? How has your faith increased in the waiting times?

_____

_____

_____

_____

_____

_____

_____

_____

_____

_____

Be strong and courageous.
Do not be afraid or terrified because of them,
for the Lord your God goes with you;
he will never leave you nor forsake you.

DEUTERONOMY 31:6

$\mathcal{O}$ur daughter Jessica was born with a day planner in one hand and a suitcase in the other. She was more than willing to organize her brother, her cousins, and her classmates in the small Christian schools she attended.

Eventually Jessica set off for an inner-city Christian college where she signed on for every cross-cultural opportunity offered. Within weeks she was volunteering at a hospice that cared for babies with AIDS. The first time I visited that place with Jess, I hovered near the door, horrified at the tangibility of so many dying children. She must have read my eyes, for when she came back into the room, a child cradled to her breast, she spoke with the intensity God had placed within her.

"When I hold them, Mom, I think that there may be only seven or eight people in the whole world who get to love them, and I get to be one of them. How cool is that?"

It was the first of many times I was humbled in my daughter's presence.

Eventually Jessica's heart took her to orphanages in Jamaica, then to mission training in Germany. Then the day came when she called and told us that her next place of service would be Nias, a tiny island off the coast of Sumatra, where she and a small team would be doing tsunami relief work in an area ravaged by disease and experiencing the daily devastation of earthquakes. It was a humanitarian aid effort of heroic proportions and enormous risks. Even Jessica's usual bubbling spirits were somber.

Dan and I could only pray and wait for reports. And when the reports came in, they were not good. Jessica and the entire team were ill, some more than others. But Jess was critically ill. She was bedridden and suffering from dehydration, dysentery, high fever, and a severe case of pink eye that had penetrated her facial tissue.

Medical supplies and diagnostic tools were virtually unavailable, and the local hospital was able to provide only hydration. Jess lay for days staring at a wall, unable to move without assistance, as earthquakes shook the region. Team members had been told to flee to the rooftops during the earthquakes so that if the buildings fell, they could ride the rubble down from the top, but Jessica was so weak she could barely get to the rooftop during the almost daily quakes. After one quake, a building three doors down collapsed.

For days Jessica lay on her back staring at a crack in the wall while the earth trembled, the world around her disintegrated, disease and hunger raged, and her body failed her. She had come to Nias for the purpose of serving others, and God had rendered her useless. For days she cried out for the presence of God to surround her, and His voice was silent. On the days when she was strong enough for us to speak to her and when we could get a cell phone connection, we could hear the despair in her voice.

When she finally was able to come home, it was obvious she had been ravaged. Her gorgeous mane of auburn hair began to fall out in handfuls, and she began to experience other medical symptoms. Although she was now able to get the treatment she so badly needed, she was exhausted in ways we could not understand.

People crowded her, waiting to hear her glowing stories of missionary service, of islanders' lives touched for Christ. But her only stories were of disease, devastation, and feelings of abandonment and failure. No one was lining up to hear those. For months she struggled with a God who seemingly walked away from her in her greatest need. Dan and I prayed for her as she pulled up her Iowa roots and moved across the country to a Christian camp and retreat center and immersed herself in a new life.

Then two months later the excitement was back in her voice.

"All the time I was in Nias I was waiting for God to surround me, but He was already there with me," she said when she called one evening. "I didn't have to feel Him. The truth was that He was with me and He didn't abandon me. I know it might sound crazy, but I just figured this out."

A few weeks later a second call came. This time she wanted to talk about a new ministry opportunity that had captured her heart. "It just seems like it might be time for me to begin praying about the next place God wants me."

Sometimes the hardest thing to believe is the simplest thing, but when we discover how simple it really is, we discover the essence of faith.

Dear God, my prayer today is, "I believe. Help my unbelief." In the middle of pain and suffering, my heart cries out for answers, for proof, for evidence, for something that can make sense of the devastation that I see in the world around me. But God, You hold the keys to the history of the world and to every indignity and injustice that has ever been perpetrated, and You promise that in the end all will be made right. Father, we cling to You, knowing that we won't find those answers in this world but only by looking into Your eyes and trusting You for the future. Give me that faith, Father.

DESCRIBE A NIAS ISLAND experience in your life. Are you able to trust that God is there, even when you can't "feel" Him?

_____

_____

_____

_____

_____

_____

_____

_____

_____

_____

I sought the Lord, and he answered me;
he delivered me from all my fears.
Those who look to him are radiant;
their faces are never covered with shame.

PSALM 34:4–5

*J*anuary was a horror.

Mom's needs were escalating, and we were all exhausted. In spite of our move back to Michigan to support my dad and mom, I was learning that there simply was not enough of me to go around. Or Dan, or other family members. I consoled myself by acknowledging that at least I was no longer driving or flying from Iowa to handle appointments and crises.

We had transitioned Norman into our new home in Michigan, but time was taking its toll. His Parkinson's, strokes, peripheral neuropathy, heart condition, broken hip, and other medical conditions were progressing. Since we'd moved to Michigan, we'd been forced to navigate the waters of new agencies, social workers, support services, and doctors. It was daunting, to say the least. And as Dan shouldered more of the responsibility for his dad's medical oversight, I found myself driving the forty miles from Grand Rapids to my parents' home in Muskegon with greater and greater regularity, where my father, who had carried the weight of Mom's growing needs for so long, was sinking. The burden of twenty-four-hour care was simply too much for him. He was exhausted. And my brother and sister-in-law, Paul and Sheryl, had made numerous trips across the state to Muskegon for medical appointments, emergency room visits, and surgeries. We were all exhausted.

But while the rational part of me knew that we needed help and had even investigated services and facilities, another voice inside my head whispered accusations.

I wasn't doing enough. I was failing my parents. Some irrational and daughterly part of me told me that if I just tried harder, I could continue working full-time, caring for Norman, freelancing a second job, focusing on my marriage, and providing for my parents' needs two counties away. A voice whispered that I *should be* able to do it all, in spite of my brain lesion and fragile health. I simply had to try harder.

Close friends and accountability partners had other

things to say. And they did not whisper. Their firm and loving tones exposed truths that were difficult for me to face.

God did not have a "doing it all" measuring stick. Even Jesus took time away from meeting others' needs to refresh His spirit. The Son of God Himself delegated responsibilities to people around Him and allowed them to share in His ministry to others. I could do the same. I did not have to prove myself to my parents, my friends, my co-workers, and the world in general.

We had returned to Michigan in August. In January my father and mother and I stepped through the doors of an adult day-care center that specialized in the needs of dementia and Alzheimer's patients. It was far from easy for my father and me, but to our surprise, Mom sat down in an activity circle and participated, soon forgetting that we were even there. As I walked beside my father back to the car, I chose to acknowledge a difficult truth: that what is best for Mom may often be difficult for me. Sometimes what is best for my parents means allowing God to take from my hands things I may not be ready to lay down myself. At times loving will mean stepping back and relinquishing, as hard as that may be for me.

Gracious Father, teach me to trust You to guard my loved ones and not see that role as my sole responsibility. Help me to listen to the voice of your Holy Spirit and to deny the lies of Satan that accuse me with false guilt and shame. Help me to clearly see what You would have me do and what You would have me release to others.

WHAT LIES HAS Satan used to accuse you of false guilt in your role as a caregiver? How have you responded? What does the truth of God's Word say to counter those lies?

_____

_____

_____

_____

_____

_____

_____

_____

_____

_____

If you, then, though you are evil,
know how to give good gifts to your children,
how much more will your Father in heaven
give good gifts to those who ask Him!

MATTHEW 7:11

$\mathcal{W}$e were back in Michigan, but somehow life had not smoothed out with the transition. But, then, *smooth* is not an adjective for life I find in either the Old or New Testaments.

Norman's safety in our home was a growing concern as his balance grew more precarious. Dan and I juggled our schedules so that we could be in the house with him as much as possible.

Then, in a series of excruciating conversations and family meetings, we decided to place Mom in an assisted-living facility as near Dad as possible. He'd be able to visit her every day and sleep soundly at night, knowing that her needs were being met. We knew it was a sound decision, a right decision. It was also a painful decision.

I'm not sure who grieved the most the day we left Mom—my father, my mother, my brother, or the spouses who love us all so much. Sheryl and I drove Mom to the center after supper, and Sheryl was the warrior who stayed through the battle, sending me home when the horror of understanding rose in Mom's eyes and her cries began.

In that moment it didn't help my heart at all that the home was run by Christians or that the rooms were decorated in tasteful Victorian colors or that a languid greyhound wandered the halls to comfort the residents with his presence. It only mattered that I was leaving my mother in a nursing home and she knew it.

Mom was there for a month while something in Dad faded. It was as though a part of him skittered away before our eyes. Before the end of the month his state was so fragile we were fearful for his health and safety. Time had become my enemy. Every hour I spent teaching at the university, my dream job, was an hour my parents needed me. I had come back to Michigan to help take care of them, and I needed to give myself the freedom to do that.

In the spring I notified the university that I would be resigning my full-time position at the end of the semester. I would continue to teach occasional classes in their evening program, but I needed flexibility. I also would continue to freelance and work for nonprofits through the fund development company I was working with.

Weeks after I announced my decision, Norman fell. Within that same week, we found him accommodations at a veteran's home just six miles from our home. Days later, we'd switched his single bed to a queen to accommodate my parents. As I write, my mother is napping in my living room, and my father is puttering in the basement.

I did not feel that I was "giving up" my job at the university. Instead, I was saying *yes* to the opportunities God presented to me to be in my home with my parents while I pursued my writing.

God gives good gifts to His children. We must be careful our vision is clear to see them for what they are. Blessings. Opportunities. These *are* words I find in God's vocabulary.

Dear Lord, help me to look at the things that You have given me as blessings and opportunities, not as things I have to lay down. Help me to see that You are the giver of all good gifts and that there are good gifts in this day for me. Give me eyes to see beauty, blessing, provision, grace, and grant me a spirit that overflows with gratitude.

HAS YOUR EMPLOYMENT been affected by your caregiving?
Has it been difficult for you to maintain an attitude of grace?
How are gratitude and grace intertwined in your life?

_____

_____

_____

_____

_____

_____

_____

_____

_____

_____

Turn my heart toward your statutes
and not toward selfish gain.
Turn my eyes away from worthless things . . .
I will walk about in freedom,
for I have sought out your precepts.

PSALM 119: 36–37, 45

$\mathcal{I}$ would like to suggest, for the welfare of families everywhere, that senior citizens devise written standards of conduct for their own special station in life. After all, family members should know what to expect from their loved ones. The generation gap does not just apply to teenagers. It may start in our teen years, but it follows us all the way to our graves.

I expected that my parents' senior years would unfold according to an unwritten rulebook that both of us would understand and agree upon. But if someone wrote a guidebook on *How to Agree upon Disbursing Your Parents' House and*

Lifelong Possessions, my dad never put it on our reading lists. So one minute my parents' home and its contents were there, and the next minute, *Poof,* they were gone.

I spent a lot of time being mad during those months when my dad was selling his house. I was mad at him because he seemed to have made a snap decision. Mad that he hadn't agreed with my brother and me on what to do regarding his financial affairs. Mad that he had included the contents of his home with the purchase price, and I felt suddenly uncomfortable asking for sentimental items that were dear to me. Mad that he had set his plan in motion without first consulting family about the implications of his decision. Mad that my brother didn't live closer so I wouldn't get stuck in the middle with the details. Life pretty much had gone south everywhere because I was so busy being mad.

When the boxes were finally packed, the pictures sorted, and my anger had faded to a slow burn, I began to face the ugliness inside my heart. Why was I so angry?

I didn't have to dig far to find the answer. I was hurt. I had wanted Dad to understand that the contents of his and Mom's house were precious to me. He hadn't offered furniture to my cousin—he'd offered my life's memories at a time when memories were dearer to me than almost anything else. And I'd wanted my father to know me well enough to understand that. I didn't want logic to win out.

I wanted understanding to fill the gaping places in my heart.

In the end, I was left with an assortment of mementos and the fruit of my anger—seeds that sprouted and crowded my heart. But I knew what I needed to do. I confessed my anger as sin and faced the truth that all my needs were met in Christ.

The test of integrity and commitment to righteousness comes when we don't get what we want—when we are faced with the choice to groan, grumble, harbor bitterness, or recognize the truth that God has met all our needs in Christ, no matter what our desires may be. After our initial moments of anger, no matter the cause, we're all left with the choice to turn to God in righteousness or to turn away to lies.

It took me six months to get my eyes off everyone else and on myself, where God intended them to be in the first place. My anger cost me six months of bitterness when I could have been walking in freedom in Christ. But God redeems even our mistakes. One minute our sin is there, and the next minute, *Poof,* it's gone. That's the wonder of forgiveness.

> *Gracious heavenly Father, I cannot thank You enough for Your everlasting mercy and forgiveness poured out in my life. Every day I face the temptation to grumble and groan about*

*life, and every day You pour out fresh mercy and forgiveness
and give me the opportunity to turn to You. Father, forgive me
for my anger at the petty things of life and at the big wounds
and roots of bitterness where I struggle deeply in my soul. God
help me to see the truth that whenever I choose anger, I reject
You. May I run into Your arms today, Father, knowing that
You are waiting there to embrace me.*

HOW IS GOD moving in your heart in regard to anger and bitterness? What will it mean for you to take your eyes off everyone
and everything else and turn to God?

_____

_____

_____

_____

_____

_____

_____

_____

_____

_____

Through the Storm,
Through the Night, Lead
Me On to the Light

Keep me safe, O God, for in you I take refuge.
I said to the Lord, "You are my Lord;
apart from you I have no good thing."
As for the saints who are in the land,
they are the glorious ones in whom is all my delight.

PSALM 16:1–3

$\mathcal{I}$ am learning something new tonight—how to bask in the beauty of the present. The gift of the now has often eluded me. Too often the next destination has obscured the blessing of the present.

Mom stands beside me at the kitchen sink, meticulously stripping away the shell of a hard-boiled egg. She focuses on the task, occasionally rinsing off the tenacious bits beneath a gentle stream of water flowing from the faucet. It takes her ten minutes to pick one clean before she nestles it gently in the yellow stoneware bowl where I've placed the dozen I've already peeled.

I hand her the chopper I've rescued from her kitchen and conscripted into my meager artillery of kitchen supplies. The metal has been worn smooth by her hand, and I wonder if the grip feels familiar to her, if perhaps her fingers remember what her mind cannot. She eyes it for a moment, then raises and lowers her forearm slowly in a delicate motion that barely grazes the tissue of the eggs. She works without distraction as a CD of hymns plays softly in the background. Three-and-a-half hymns mark the time between us before she speaks.

"Am I doing this right?"

It couldn't be any more right, I assure her.

I ladle in the remaining ingredients for egg salad and place a wooden spoon in her hand. She works the mixture in wispy strokes in the center of the bowl.

"What's this?" she asks.

"Egg salad—just like you like it—with a bit of mustard, relish, and Miracle Whip."

"I didn't know I liked egg salad."

"You do."

I watch silently for a few more moments as she stirs.

"What's this?"

"It's egg salad, Mom."

She reaches into the sink where the broken shells lay.

"Do you want these in there?"

"Not today, Mom."

Ten minutes later, the egg salad is finished. It is the crowning achievement of the day, the week, the month. It is a moment of shared delight that will never again be duplicated. It is the gift of the now that even in the making has become a gift for forever.

I am storing up the egg salad moments—hoarding them like sweets in the hand of a child. Each day is a scavenger hunt. Each sight, sound, memory—a treasure.

The scent of Oil of Olay as I work its silky texture into my mother's arms and legs.

The gentle arch of her shoulders as I massage her back after a bath.

Her raised eyebrows and smile when I offer her ice cream.

They are all daily lessons in basking in the moment—small gifts of the present that will sustain me in the future. Gifts of constant, daily provision to sustain and strengthen my heart. Gifts from God. Good things in the midst of the hard things. Glorious things disguised as the mundane and the incidental.

I only wish that the basking lessons had begun sooner, that I had learned in my younger years to recognize that what appears to be mundane and insignificant always nestles in the palm of the eternal. It is a truth that makes even the scent of egg salad a reason for thanks.

Father God, give me a heart skilled in basking in moments of pleasure with my loved ones—whether those moments be with those I serve by giving care or with my family and friends. You created me with a heart that needs these moments to nurture my spirit, and I thank You for gifts of beauty and laughter and pleasure. Teach me to bask in Your love and Your presence each and every moment of my day, regardless of how difficult the circumstances appear to me. No matter the difficulty of my day, may I continue to find moments of delight in my caregiving.

LIST A FEW OF your "egg salad" treasures. They may be memories, scents, scenes, or sounds. What makes these things special to you?

_____

_____

_____

_____

_____

_____

_____

_____

_____

_____

𝒟arkness is pressing in, and she is growing restless. My mother paces my living room floor, weeping and tormented, compelled by the forces that grip her relentlessly in the evening hours.

The doctors call it sundowning. We have other words for it, this tentacle of Alzheimer's that ravages my mother's mind and pulls her behind a locked door each night. We do not have a key, but we have light, and we have found ways to shine its glimmering brilliance beneath the door. Sometimes she sees it, sometimes she does not, but it is always there. Even in moments when it does not comfort her, the light comforts us.

The light of Truth. The light of a sovereign God who was and is and is to come.

I take my mother's hand and draw her down the dim hallway and into the bedroom she shares with my father, who waits on the couch for the stilling of her whimpering. Perhaps the reality of his own physical frailty pounds its rhythm in his broken heart. His head rests lightly on the back of the couch as if he is sleeping. I know he is not.

I ease Mom's head to the pillow and draw the covers beneath her chin as I whisper words of comfort. She is cold. She sobs as she tells me. It seems she is always cold these days. In just a moment you will be warm, I assure her. And yes, I will stay. I always stay.

I settle cross-legged on the floor beside her, taking her hand in my own as I press the button on the CD player. Soothing strings and haunting woodwinds fill the air, and her shoulders relax. I breathe deeply and stare into her eyes as I sing.

"Precious Lord, take my hand,
Lead me on, help me stand.
I am tired, I am weak, I am worn.
Through the storm, through the night
Lead me on to the light.
Take my hand, precious Lord,
Lead me home."

My voice trembles, but she does not notice.

"That's beautiful," she whispers to me. She smiles, and I know she has seen the glimmers. The sobs fade and the tremors ease. Once again, the light has shown beneath the door, and I am grateful.

"Yes," I smile back through tears. "It's beautiful."

The moments of precious brilliance shimmer in my own heart, and I hoard them away—hoard them away to wield in future struggles with my own darkness.

There is nothing I cherish more than the moments of peace I share with my mother. The moments when I take her hand in my own, and our two hands together are clasped in the hand of God.

> *God, engulf me, devour me in the light of Your presence. May it permeate every fiber of my life in ways that sustain and nourish those around me and point them to You. May I be consumed with the brilliance of who You are.*

IN WHAT WAYS has God shown you the brightness of His face, even in the darkest hours of your caregiving? What beauty have you found in your journey as a caregiver?

_____

_____

_____

_____

_____

The eternal God is your refuge,
and underneath are the everlasting arms.

DEUTERONOMY 33:27

$\mathcal{I}$t has been a night of weeping and wandering. I sit beside Mom on the couch fingering the edges of the soft blanket draped around her shoulders, watching as the pale wash of a winter dawn seeps through the darkness and tinges the room.

It began hours before, with quiet sobs for a pain she cannot name and I cannot determine to be real, imagined, or a surreal magnification of an insignificant bruise or bump. Dan is away on a retreat, and I move her from my father's bed to my own, gifting him with the luxury of uninterrupted rest.

Over the next two hours I muster every remedy in my arsenal—meds, massage, heat, and hymns, but the sobs do not subside. They wear at my heart, and soon I move Mom from the bed and ease her into the soft cushions of a re-cliner, tucking the heating pad behind her and cocooning the blankets around her legs and shoulders as I pray for the crying to cease.

My prayers are answered, and for nearly an hour she rests quietly as we watch reruns of *Andy Griffith*. She likes Barney best, and twice she laughs out loud. I laugh with her. I love Barney, too. I would love him even more if he were on all night.

Her interest in television fades as the program changes, and she struggles from her chair and stands.

"I have to get out of here. I have to go home."

"This is home, Mom."

She raises her hand, and my heart flinches as I anticipate the slap that does not come. In its place, stinging words pour across my face. Something inside me whispers that I have failed once again to comfort her, that if I had only used the right words, spoken in the right tone, given her the right pill, she wouldn't have to suffer in this way.

The pacing begins, a circuit around the living room, down the hall, and through the kitchen, accompanied by a quiet monologue of random phrases. I move in front of her and barricade the door to the basement steps, hoping she doesn't realize it is a defensive move. But the hostility has dissipated, like a fog receding on the horizon, and I have become a mere shadow among the shadows. For hours we pace, repeating the circuit until she settles silently again into a corner of the couch. Again I wrap her in blankets and sink into the cushions beside her as I wait for her to quiet and drift into sleep.

In the past weeks I, too, have been pacing in my heart, retracing the lies that so easily delude my sense of reality in the midst of the suffering and the weariness and the waiting.

Lies born out of weariness and doubt.

Lies birthed from a heart that wants all pain eased and all struggle erased. Not necessarily in the world, but in my corner of it.

Lies about a loving God who allows His children to suffer. My faith doesn't allow me to speak the lies out loud, but I recognize their rising and falling rhythms pulsating through my days.

In the weariness and doubt, I raise my hand toward heaven with an outpouring of stinging words as I trace my own circles of questioning and confusion.

But as I grasp a small corner of the blanket that drapes my mother's body, I am overwhelmed by a vision of Jesus walking beside me as I mutter and stumble. Arms outstretched, He barricades the path of self-pity and ingratitude that beckons me. My moans wear at His heart, and I am cocooned in His love in spite of my own delusions. He never wearies, sleeps, or slumbers. He knows tomorrow, and He has already made provision for it. Even tonight, as I trace my mother's footsteps, He walks beside me and is my refuge.

The tears that come with that truth wash away all others that have gone before.

Dear Father, You know I try to hide my doubts and fears from others, and You have asked me to bring those doubts and fears to You. You alone know the incredible difficulty of my journey of caregiving. But You alone have provided all that I need for each day. God, give me strength in my weariness. Give me faith that sustains me in times of doubt. Give me a growing sense each day of Your unfailing love. Be my refuge, O Father. May I trust in Your everlasting arms, which bear me up in the moments when I feel most faint.

WHAT DOUBTS AND fears have you struggled with? How has God met you in those moments? What Scripture promises have helped you in your times of struggle?

_____

_____

_____

_____

_____

_____

But I trust in you, O Lord;
I say, "You are my God."
My times are in your hands.

PSALM 31:14–15

$\mathcal{I}$ can see the question in my friends' eyes before they even speak the words.

"How long can you keep doing this?"

For years the question meant, "How long can you take care of Norman?" Now it's directed toward Mom and Dad.

Our answer has always been the same. "We're not sure, but we'll do it as long as we can."

"And how will you know how long that is?"

It's a good question. Dan and I just know that when the time comes, we'll know. We know that when we've done all God has called us to do, He will tell us what the next step will look like.

When we first learned Norman was struggling with depression and mental illness, we knew we could help him in our home. But when his needs surpassed our ability to keep him safe and healthy, we made the difficult decision to place him in a psychiatric hospital. When he was well enough to be discharged, we brought him home again.

After he broke his hip and completed rehab in a nursing center, we brought him home again.

And after he had a stroke and completed rehab once again, we brought him home.

Each time he went into the nursing home for rehab or respite stays, we saw the fear in his eyes—the fear that maybe this time he wouldn't be coming home. His stays there were especially difficult because of his thirst for solitude. We were honest with him, telling him that we would make every effort to keep him with us as long as possible, but we had to know he was safe in our home and that we could meet his needs there.

When we moved back to Michigan from Iowa, Norman's transition was difficult. We placed him in a nursing home until we got settled. Then, when we tried to enroll him for services that would help us keep him in our home, we found that Michigan simply did not have the resources Iowa had to help us with his care. We were able to keep him in our home for eight months before we realized that he needed twenty-four-hour care that we could not provide.

Our decision to move back to Michigan to help my parents had directly impacted our ability to care for Norman. It didn't seem fair.

But we do not live in a world where fair prevails. And I, for one, am eternally grateful that God does not apply a standard of fairness but a standard of mercy in His relationship with me. I must remember that I am never to expect fairness in a world of injustice, imbalance, and sin. I am simply to be a stalk of wheat whose roots go deeply among the tares of the world.

It was a spring afternoon when our friend Mishele stopped by to check on Dad Beach and found him crumpled in the hallway where he had fallen. It was the second of his falls in just a few weeks. By that Friday we were able to place him at a veteran's facility just seven miles from our home.

We hadn't even known the facility existed prior to Norman's fall, but God provided exactly the right convergence of people, information, available space, and funding to make it possible for him to be in a facility that provided for all of his needs. There he found Christian chaplains who faithfully preached the Word each Sunday, fellow believers, and even a roommate who shared a passion for Christ.

How long can Dan and I care for my parents in our home? I don't know, but God has the days numbered, and He will tell us. He has told us to listen and watch for the signs, and I know that when the time comes, He has already prepared the way for the next step for them.

> *Dear gracious Father, thank You for not applying a standard of fairness to my life but granting mercy and favor when I do not deserve it. Help me to realize that I do not serve others out of obligation or desire for reward or goodness but simply to honor them and to honor You. Give me the wisdom to know when I must relinquish my care to someone else or, when the time comes, to transition my loved one to care that is better for them. Help me to let go, and free my heart from false guilt. Help me to live in freedom, Lord, knowing that You have already prepared the way for the next step for them.*

HAS IT BEEN difficult for you to think about or discuss "next steps" with family members or loved ones? What kinds of things regarding your loved one's situation or your own situation will tell you that those steps need to be taken? Do you struggle with false guilt over decisions like these? Consider talking to a pastor or counselor about those areas.

_____

_____

_____

_____

_____

Finally, all of you, live in harmony with one another;
be sympathetic, love as brothers, be compassionate and humble.

1 PETER 3:8

$\mathcal{A}$ few years ago if you had told me that I would be decorating with garbage, I would have said you were crazy. But that's where God's brought me, and I'm proud of it.

Nobody told me caregiving would be about boundaries, about who you are and about who your parents are, about where you draw the lines of separation between yourselves, about how you define honor and respect. A lot of caregivers are unprepared for boundary issues (like I was), and it can make their experience difficult, awkward, or even excruciating.

My dad and I have always been pretty different. He likes to be up at the crack of dawn. I believe the crack of dawn is highly overrated. He checks his tire pressure weekly. When I see I have a flat, I'm pretty sure my tire pressure is low. He walks through fast food drive-thrus collecting scattered change. I hide in the restroom and pretend I don't know him.

Dad is direct when he speaks. (Saying this is like saying that Bill Gates has a little money.) So when Mom and Dad moved into our house, we had a ready-made recipe for disaster just waiting. I was going to continue to do my stuff in my own way in my own home, like fifty-year-old women do, and Dad was going to have to learn to live with my way of doing things.

The list of things my father does that I find irksome could fill its own book. But one of the most annoying is his habit of taking my garbage bags out of the wastebasket and hooking them to my kitchen cabinets until we gather enough trash to fill the bags to the very top so that not an iota of space will be wasted and we will not be guilty of wasting 2.7 cents on an extra bag. Since I do not appreciate half-filled garbage bags taking up floor space in my kitchen on a daily basis, I told my father so—graciously and quietly—at an appropriate moment. It seemed to be an appropriate boundary for me to lay down at the time. And, surprisingly, Dad complied without comment.

What I learned over the next few weeks as the Holy Spirit directed my heart toward my attitudes toward my garbage bags and my motives was that boundaries really don't have a lot to do with garbage bags. They have to do with respect, honor, and integrity. Garbage bags were only a symptom. What Dad and I needed to work at was communicating respect and honor to one another and to begin discussing appropriate boundaries for our living situation.

For a fifty-year-old little girl and an eighty-four-year-old father, this can be mind-boggling hard work. But we're taking it one day at a time, one baby step at a time, one glorious new level of respect at a time.

This morning a garbage bag is looped to my kitchen cabinets. I barely notice it any more. I've learned that it can actually be pretty handy to loop them there while you fill them up. One afternoon a few weeks ago I noticed Dad taking a half-filled bag and stashing it in my kitchen pantry closet. When I asked him why he was moving it, his answer surprised and delighted me.

"Because I know you have some friends coming over in a little while and I know women don't like decorating with garbage."

Thank you, Dad. I think we're both growing up.

Dear God, give me wisdom to see the difference between healthy boundaries and hanging onto things that don't matter. Give me the freedom to be able to lay down things that don't count and the tenacity to fight for things that do count. Help me to recognize those things in my heart that have kept me a child and to grow past those wounds into a healthy adult. Show me how to respect and honor my loved one in all things, and draw us together in a new bond of unity.

IN WHAT AREAS DO you still struggle with childish perceptions and expectations of yourself? How do you think God would like to change your heart in these areas?

_____

_____

_____

_____

_____

_____

_____

_____

_____

_____

*Do you know how God controls the clouds
and makes his lightning flash?
Do you know how the clouds hang poised,
those wonders of him who is perfect in knowledge?*

JOB 37:15–16

The first time I sat in a marriage class taught by Louie, our pastor, and heard him speak about a woman's compulsion to control her husband, I thought I might collapse. I thought perhaps someone had sent him an e-mail about my life and revealed my darkest family secrets. I had heard scary stories about this guy, how he was known to ask pointed questions and press people for honest answers.

I was into honesty and transparency—to a degree. Because I knew, of course, that if anyone truly knew who I was, they would stamp the word *Rejected* on my forehead and run the other way.

When I heard Louie's comment about control, I broke

out in a cold sweat because I have long had a major compulsion to control *everything*. I've been perfectly willing to tip my hat to the Lord and acknowledge that He is sovereign, but I've never been willing to do the hard work of learning to abide and rest.

The grace of God and Louie's verbal baseball bat to the head helped me realize that my compulsion to control was a sin. This process of revelation in my life has been painful and progressive, but God continues to be patient with me. I'm convinced my husband will have his own zip code in heaven someday—somewhere near John the Baptist and Moses—just for putting up with me.

Control issues are a problem for someone who has taken on the task of helping frail parents walk through their final days because there are far too many things a caregiver can feel compelled to control. Spouses. Family members. The person they're responsible for caring for. Doctors. The entire medical community. The insurance industry. People who design handicap stalls. Friends struggling to know how to show support. The disease. Their own health. Their job. Their boss. The number of hours in a day. The rate at which gray hairs grow.

The secret to breaking free from control addiction is much simpler than we would like to think. For me it's boiled down to one simple thing: to ask myself the question, *Why do you feel you need to do this?* The responses I give first are often self-delusional. I usually feel I must change the person or the circumstances, but that can never be my goal. My goal must always be to minister love to everyone else while giving God the work of changing my heart.

I have come to realize that it's not always my job to *do* it, *change* it, *initiate* it, *plan* it, or *take responsibility* for it. Often, if I haven't examined my true motives and bathed them in prayer, I'm stepping out of God's time frame or I'm stepping into someone else's area of responsibility.

I've learned that God often works in the spaces. I've spent too much of my time running ahead, filling in the gaps, and sputtering through the quiet times. But God asks us to *be still and know Him.* For me, this means sitting back and waiting to see what He will do while I simply pray and wait.

I've also learned that God speaks in the stillness. I've learned to pour over Scripture and suck the truth from its rich soil. As I do, my roots go deep, and I learn the secrets of abiding.

When I'm still enough to ponder the clouds poised above my head, I'm able to rest in a knowledge too wide and too deep for me to attain. In those moments I rest in the knowledge that the name written upon my forehead is not *Rejected*, but *Embraced.*

Dear God, forgive me for my attempts to control the people and circumstances around me for my own purposes. You know that daily I face frustrations that stretch me beyond my own ability to cope. Give me a burning desire for roots that go deep and to know the secrets of abiding in You. Give me the faith to trust You to work in the spaces and in the stillness. In this very moment, quiet my heart and let me feel the warmth of Your embrace as I face this day.

WHAT WILL IT MEAN for you to relinquish control to God? In what particular areas do you struggle with control? How can you work to create "spaces" and "stillness" in your life?

_____

_____

_____

_____

_____

_____

_____

_____

_____

_____

*Therefore confess your sins to each other
and pray for each other so that you may be healed.
The prayer of a righteous man is powerful and effective.*

JAMES 5:16

⌒he phone rings at 11:10 p.m. and I reach to answer it as I'm scrunching into bed beside Dan. Once again I'm exhausted and already beginning to make my mental list for the next day.

"Where were you at 10:30 when I called the first time, and how many hours' sleep have you been getting these past few weeks, young lady?"

I feel, simultaneously, a flush of excitement for being called *young lady* and a sense of teenage shame for having violated a curfew I didn't know I had. It is the voice of my neurologist, a man who has cared for me for seven years and who knows every detail of my health and my life. He is returning a call that I placed to him the day before regarding old neurological symptoms that seem to have returned. He knows I only call when I am concerned, and he knows that when I am concerned I tend to obsess about my symptoms. I could choose a more spiritual word to describe how I respond when my brain abnormalities pop up like some kind of neurological *Whack-a-Mole* game, but *obsess* is closer to the truth.

Dr. Barger holds a special place in my life, along with a number of other individuals. They are my mirror bearers—people responsible for making me look deeply at myself, beyond the superficialities and the schedules to what is often so hard for me to see on my own.

My weaknesses.

My obsessions.

My excuses.

My self-delusions and lies.

My accountability group holds the mirror before me every two weeks. These no-nonsense women ask the tough questions about everything from my relationships with family members to my marriage and my weight. They delve into my heart and help me evaluate my motives when I most want to see myself as a victim. They force me to ask *Why?* when I want to gloss over my attitudes and focus on the actions that make me look good. They're a tough crowd, but anybody who wants to grow needs a tough crowd who loves Jesus to help them do a little weeding. Without them,

I could not experience the kind of inside-out life change that Christ expects of me.

My church also holds up a mirror through its teaching and small group ministry. It has been painful, and it has been exhilarating, and it has carried Dan and me through the darkest days of our caregiving. We have learned what it is to be gloriously loved with love that is unconditional and gives without regard for what can or will be given in return. We have learned that repentance, faith, and forgiveness are a lifestyle. We have learned that we should not be surprised to stand in the place of suffering, and that suffering serves to reveal the mysteries of God.

I am grateful for my mirror bearers. I would be a fool to refuse to turn my head when they direct my face toward my weaknesses, my excuses, my lies, and my sins. They are God's gift to me. Even in the middle of the night.

Dear Father God, You know that it's my nature to turn away from my weaknesses, faults, and sins. You love me deeply, in spite of these things, yet You desire to change me more and more into the image of Your Son. When the mirror bearers in my life reflect truth, give me the wisdom and grace to look and listen, dear Father. Place them about me in abundance and give me ears to listen and eyes to see Your truth as it is spoken. Change my heart, Lord, and give me a spirit that thirsts for renewal in You.

WHAT PEOPLE SERVE as "mirror bearers" in your life? Do you feel as though you need more people serving you in this way? What resources are available to you through your church or Christian friends to develop your circle of mirror bearers?

_____

_____

_____

_____

_____

_____

_____

_____

_____

_____

I will lie down and sleep in peace,
for you alone, O Lord, make me dwell in safety.

PSALM 4:8

$\mathcal{O}$nce again I am sliding into an MRI tube, the cold sides pressing tightly against my elbows as I grip the panic ball that rests lightly in my right hand. Dan waits in my hospital room for my return from yet another test for the stroke-like symptoms that have been washing over me with waves of weakness and numbness for three days. For three days my neurologist has been telling me to go to the emergency room. For three days I have refused, knowing that my history will qualify me for one of every test in the medical books. And who will take care of my parents and check on Norman, who seems to be showing signs of pneumonia? I have too many responsibilities to be ill.

But a spell last night left me prostrate on my bed for nearly an hour as my blood pressure skyrocketed, then plummeted. I could barely speak or walk as Dan made the decision for me. I was going. He quietly gathered my things and made plans for friends to check on Mom and Dad and bring them meals as I sobbed out my guilt for causing us yet another medical expense.

I have had dozens of MRIs, but this time I haven't had the chance to prepare my "List of Warm and Wonderful Things to Think About" to distract me in that cold, narrow place. The memory of once being tied and swaddled in my bedsheets with my head clamped in a cage while the techs left me unattended still haunts me. It was only for minutes, but it seemed that for hours I lay entombed and unable to move in that horrible place. With each new MRI, this fearful memory threatens to overtake me, and the list has always been my defense. But they have brought me too soon this time, and I am afraid I will panic.

I am embarrassed for my mumbled apologies to the tech as she wheels me toward the procedure room. I am ashamed that I must remove my glasses and squeeze my eyes tightly shut.

"I can't look at the hole. If I see how small it is, I'll lose it. If you could just back me in and help me onto the table . . ."

I know my unwillingness to look at the tube is a game I play only with myself and has nothing to do with reality. I am old enough and wise enough to know that how I feel does not influence what is true.

I am in an MRI tube, and I am safe, I tell myself. It is truth. Nothing is going to harm me. For the next thirty-two minutes, I will rest in perfect safety while someone watches over me. No matter how frightening the sounds that pound at my brain, I am in a place of protection. The only thing that can threaten me in this place is my own fear, and my fear is founded on perceptions and not realities.

Too often my fears are based upon perceptions and not realities. That my needs will not be met. That God is not in control. That He is not enough. That what is important and what is eternal can be measured by what I can see around me. These are the lies that press in upon me in the closed, narrow, cold spaces of life.

Today I will choose to close my eyes and rest in the tube. My parents are not alone at home. Dan and I are not alone in our caregiving. Underneath are the everlasting arms, keeping me safe and secure. I may choose to shut my eyes tightly and back into the frightening spaces of my life, but I can rest assured that God goes before me and surrounds me in all things. He alone is my safety and security. He alone is my place of shelter and refuge.

Gracious God, today may I look into Your face and see only Your eyes of love for me. I choose to bathe my heart in the truth that my safety and security lie in You. Even when my circumstances seem out of control, You are there, bearing me up and giving me strength. Father, give me rest today, rest in body, soul, and spirit. Revive my heart and refresh my body. May I find peace and comfort in knowing that You are always there to shelter and protect me.

IN WHAT AREAS of your life as a caregiver is it difficult for you to rest? What truth of Scripture can you turn to to redirect your heart into truth?

_____

_____

_____

_____

_____

_____

_____

_____

_____

My grace is sufficient for you,
for my power is made perfect in weakness.

2 CORINTHIANS 12:9

The call comes at eleven o'clock at night. Mom has just settled back down after a trip to the bathroom, and Dad has crawled in bed beside her after guiding her through the hallway, his CPAP* machine clinging to his head like an errant squid. Dan is preparing for bed, and I am lying back against the pillows trying to ignore the migraine that pounds through my brain. How ironic that the anti-seizure medication the doctors have prescribed for my headaches has induced an unrelenting, skull-splitting headache. The pharmacist has told me to expect it to last from ten to fourteen days. I am on day four, and I am considering removing my pharmacist from my Christmas list.

---

*Continuous positive airway pressure, to stimulate normal breathing during sleep.

The moment I hear Julia's voice, I expect the worst. She is the night nurse at the veteran's home. Before I speak two words, I signal Dan to put his clothes back on. Norman's lungs are filling. Yes, we will meet the ambulance at the hospital. We can be there in thirty minutes.

I do not have time to give in to the wave of desperation that washes over me. I can only put one foot in front of the other and do the next thing. I have been out of the hospital for five days. My doctors have told me that my stress level is too high, and it is affecting my health. I have not had a full night's sleep since I have been home from the hospital. Mom has been restless, and most nights I've floated between the couch and the bed in my office. Episodes of numbness drift through my body, my blood pressure has grown erratic, and waves of weakness threaten to take me to my knees at the most unexpected times.

I do not remember the ride to the hospital. I do remember standing at the rear of the ambulance as Norman is unloaded into the cold night air, a blanket wrapped tightly around him and an oxygen mask strapped to his head. He is blue-gray. I stroke his face as he is wheeled past me.

In the emergency room I settle onto a stool beside Dan and watch through one slitted eye as the trauma team administers breathing treatments and assessments. My head continues to pound. I wonder if there is a drug nearby that someone could inject me with. I cannot remember if

I took my evening medications before I left the house. I wonder if I have remembered to pack a snack for myself and when the last time was that I ate. I am diabetic and envision myself slumping onto the floor in a giant throbbing, perspiring lump.

For the next four hours we sit at Norman's side, and I close my eyes tight against the brightness and the sounds of the room. I retreat to the place inside myself where I keep my "Guilt List." Tonight the list is enormous. I feel guilty that I am not standing at Norman's side, giving him more comfort, but instead am slumped against the wall succumbing to pain that has beaten me down. I feel guilty that I am not supporting my husband but am leaning into his side, exhausted. I feel guilty that I am not home with my parents, and that when I am home I cannot stave off their increasing needs or even meet the ones that are already there. I feel guilty that my body is succumbing to stress when "strong Christians" do not succumb to stress.

I know that this place is a place of my own making, constructed of lies I have chosen to believe because of my wounds. God does not expect me to be sufficient in all things. He does not expect me to be the Great Physician, the Comforter. He has given me the luxury of being weak so that He can be glorified in showing His strength. He reminds me in that moment, as I sit slumped against the wall, that in my weakness I am to find rest in the truth.

Tonight that truth is that, in spite of my weaknesses, I am at Norman's side, clinging to Dan's hand. My parents are safe in my home, and their needs are met. And in spite of a pounding headache, God has given me strength to take the steps I have needed to take today.

Even with a migraine, this is reason for praise.

Dear Lord, often I am so exhausted in my caregiving, and I don't know where the strength will come from to complete the next task, but You have promised me Your strength in my weakness. Drive me into Your Word to find power to combat the lies of guilt that flow from the wounded places in my spirit. Make me mighty in the inward places of my heart.

WHAT REVIVES YOUR spirit in your moments of exhaustion? How has God used people or experiences to minister to you when you felt you couldn't take the next step? How have you been used to minister in the lives of others in this way?

_____

_____

_____

_____

_____

_____

_____

Create in me a pure heart, O God,
and renew a steadfast spirit within me . . .
Grant me a willing spirit, to sustain me . . .
The sacrifices of God are a broken spirit;
a broken and contrite heart, O God, you will not despise.

PSALM 51:10, 12, 17

$\mathscr{I}$ surveyed the pile of books beside my chair, books on
parent care a friend had brought me earlier that day. "They
have lots of good information for your research on family
caregiving issues," she'd said.

I'd smiled when she'd handed them to me. My brother
and I and our two spouses were totally devoted to my parents, to each other, and to God. Our children had been
raised with Grandma, Grandpa, and aunts and uncles as the
go-to babysitters. To celebrate a holiday, birthday, or wedding without everyone there was unthinkable. Members of
our family practically shared toothbrushes.

But what I hadn't shared openly over the years were the secret places of my heart.

My frustrations.

My childhood wounds.

My inadequacies and fears.

I'd smiled politely at my friend and taken the books, aware of the dark nooks and crannies into which I'd swept the debris and tried to hide it from the eyes of loved ones and friends.

But the Enemy is not blind to the dark corners where our motives, wounds, self-deception, and pride lie hidden like spiritual dust bunnies. And caregiving can be a lot like pulling out the family refrigerator for the first time in twenty years.

Suddenly our deepest struggles can lie exposed and embedded in the gunk and grime of life for all the world to see. Or at least those closest to us.

I reached for the books beside me and sorted through them until my fingers closed around the one I knew would hold the answers. I opened my Bible to Psalm 51 and prayed—words that I knew would not come without a price.

I prayed for a broken spirit. A willing spirit. A steadfast spirit. I prayed for the honesty and discernment to look deeply into my heart for roots of frustration, bitterness, anger, jealousy, and to ask the Spirit of God to focus a searchlight upon ungodly attitudes and lies.

My attitudes.

My lies.

My false motives.

In the months to come I would be driven to Psalm 51 again and again. I would learn that brokenness requires hard work, tears, and commitment on a moment-by-moment basis. It requires saturating my spirit with the Word and reminding myself again and again that God honors a broken and contrite spirit, and that He has promised to empower us. Our despair is sometimes His best tool to clean out the grime in our hearts and create something new.

Love boldly. Break easily. And give God nothing less than a pure heart.

Dear Father God, You know my heart more intimately than I know it myself. Give me eyes to see and wisdom to discern the sinful, selfish, prideful things there that dishonor and grieve You. Perhaps they are things deeply rooted in my past, my childhood, or lies about who I am or who You see me to be. Father, I commit my heart, words, actions, and my life to honoring You in all things. Give me the wisdom to walk in truth and to commit to preserve spiritual and emotional life and health in all my dealings with my loved ones.

WHAT BRICKS OF separation have been put up between your family members over the years? What heart work might God have you do to help bring about reconciliation and restoration? What things is God asking you to change that could bring greater emotional and spiritual health to those around you?

_____

_____

_____

_____

_____

_____

_____

_____

_____

_____

_____

Take My Hand, Precious Lord, Lead Me Home

Even when I am old and gray,
do not forsake me, O God,
till I declare your power to the next generation,
your might to all who are to come.

PSALM 71:18

I am speaking to my son Nathan on the phone as he describes his current girlfriend. He assures me that we will have much in common when we meet. I try to envision the woman he describes, and I wonder if she is the woman he will someday marry. I pray that, if she is, she will have medical knowledge, a love of books, and an aversion to country music.

"You are going to find a wife who will love your dad and me to death, won't you, my dear?" I quip.

I am painfully aware that my daughter Jessica will probably be living out her life in a yurt on the remote edges of civilization. Even though her last mission trip doing tsunami relief almost killed her, my heart tells me she will be headed out again soon. I know my daughter loves me, but I don't want to live out my final years with a squat toilet. So I'm bold enough to be asking God outright for a daughter-in-law who will love me a whole lot.

We laugh again, but my throat is tight. The reality of my future looms with stark reality. I already suffer from a rather banged-up brain and a memory that has all the retaining qualities of a colander. My mother has Alzheimer's, and my father's memory has been labeled deficient. Grandma Stewart suffered from dementia, as well, and I would tell you how bad Grandpa Stewart's memory was if I could just remember him. My gene pool appears to be more of a mud puddle, medically speaking.

To admit that I struggle with fear seems unspiritual. But, truth be told, the fear is there, flickering in the shadows. The possibility of Alzheimer's is a stark reality for me, and I find myself sifting the routine of life for its glimmers. I evaluate my idiosyncrasies, wondering if they are beginning to stray toward the eccentric. I ponder the moments when I call the refrigerator a typewriter and fret over the daily search for things I have misplaced. At times I feel fingers of panic grip me when I recognize someone and have no knowledge of who they are.

My comfort for the future comes from the provision of the past. The God who has so faithfully carried me through life will carry me through death. My prayer is that whatever my final days may hold for me, I will make every opportunity to tell of God's faithfulness in my life.

I will not be forsaken in my old age. God will sustain me, as He always has. My prayer is that I might use every experience, every joy, every sorrow, to make His name known to those around me, and that moments of fear would drive me to know Him more.

Precious Father, Your Word tells me that perfect love casts out fear and that those who know You have no need to fear. Help me to know Your love more intimately and with greater abandon. May I use each day to proclaim Your grace, Your mercy, and Your awesome love to generations to come.

WHAT ELEMENTS OF fear have you experienced and how have you dealt with that fear? What lessons of God's faithfulness can you share with your loved ones and family? How does God's provision in the past provide assurance for your future?

_____

_____

_____

_____

_____

_____

For God, who said, "Let light shine out of darkness,"
made his light shine in our hearts
to give us the light of the knowledge of the glory of
God in the face of Christ.

2 CORINTHIANS 4:6

The night air is sharp, the cold burning my fingertips with hot pinpricks as I pull out of the hospital parking lot and head through the darkened streets of the city. I reach for the controls of the heater and adjust the knobs, knowing that there will be no warmth until I pass the pizzeria near Division Street. On milder nights I have felt the first breaths of comfort within a few blocks of the hospital, but not tonight. I slide my right hand beneath my thigh to keep it warm.

It is Dan's turn to stay with his father. Sue and Jeff, Dan's sister and brother-in-law, will follow me home soon. They have stayed behind for a few final moments with

Norman, moments of gentle ministrations, words of comfort, whispered memories. He is growing weaker and his breathing more labored. The doctor has made it clear that there is no hope for recovery.

Earlier today we gathered around Norman's bed and asked him to sign a Do Not Resuscitate order. The doctor has told us that his frail body would not survive CPR, that the chest compressions would most likely break his fragile bones. He has described in vivid detail the trauma of resuscitation to prolong Norman's life. Norman does not want a ventilator—he has expressed that desire clearly, and it has become our task to make him now see the futility of CPR.

The silence, like so many silences in Norman's life, has been loud and prolonged as we gather around the bed. Sue and Jeff stand near his head, and Sue clasps his hand gently in her own. Dan is seated in a chair at Norman's side, his hand resting lightly on his father's leg. I stand at the foot of the bed.

The conversation is halted, awkward. It seems as though we are asking the man we love to simply give up and die. Perhaps that is what we are asking him to do. He has always sought, above all things, to do what is right. Even in this moment, he is searching to know what is right.

His eyes flutter closed briefly, and he finds his answer.

"Tell them not to do CPR."

I turn onto the interstate and head north toward home.

The heater is puffing its first feeble breaths of warmth. I reach my hand toward the vent and rotate my fingers in the tepid stream of air as I glance toward home. A pale amber glow burns in the northwest sky. I scan the horizon and spot a second pillar of light, then a third as I make my way north.

By the time I reach my exit, I'm fascinated. I turn west, then north again and drive slowly through a crystalline fog that has enveloped my car. Every light in my path has become an amber beacon, reflecting into the night sky with a surreal radiance.

A porch light glows with haloed rings of white.

Headlights from an approaching car nearly blind me with their intensity.

Circling spotlights from the nearby airport shimmer in a psychedelic light show.

The intense cold has transformed invisible crystals into tiny refractors that cast light upward in a heavenly dance.

I suddenly realize the truth.

Norman is giving up nothing and gaining everything. We are inviting him to join in the heavenly dance, to allow himself to be blinded with the intensity of the nearness of glory, and to gain comfort from the lights approaching on the horizon. We are asking him to let go of the dimness of this world for the brilliance of the next. And that is the best thing we could ever ask of him. The heavenly lights are his invitation and our assurance.

Dear Father, sometimes the best thing we can ever do for our loved one is to tell them that it's all right to go home to be with You. We want so much to keep them with us for as long as possible, but we know that life here on earth can mean suffering and pain. Give me the courage to be able to tell my loved one good-bye when the time comes, to make my parting words loving and sweet. Give me wisdom to know what to say and when to say it—not for my sake, but for theirs.

WHAT WORDS OF love do you want to express to your loved one before their passing? Have you taken the opportunity to begin expressing these things? How can you begin to prepare for the time of their death?

_____

_____

_____

_____

IF YOUR LOVED ONE doesn't know the Lord, what do you think God would have you say to them? How can you minister Christ's love in their life in ways that they can see and feel?

_____

_____

_____

_____

Weeping may remain for a night,
but rejoicing comes in the morning.

PSALM 30:5B

$\mathcal{I}$ have sunk deeply into an overstuffed plaid couch. I can't imagine a resident at the veteran's home who could possibly extricate themselves once they committed to this man-eating monstrosity. Dan sits beside me, oblivious to physical discomfort. He is staring out the window, past his sister and brother-in-law, to the barren oaks that provide a backdrop for a mammoth American flag in the warmer months. It is February. There is no flag today.

Dan's father is dying. Sue, Jeff, Dan, and I are waiting for the doctor and the hospice nurse to come. We know what they will say before they speak the words. That they will make Norman's passing as comfortable as possible. That the time is short—days, perhaps hours. That the gurglings and gaspings that seem so gruesome to us are unknown to him. I wonder if their reassurances will be simply words of comfort or are perhaps based on some bizarre scientific study. I would take comfort in a scientific study right now.

After a week of tag-team vigils, sleepless nights, random meals, hallway conferences, musical beds, adrenaline highs, and emotional lows, the four of us are silent and still, alone in one another's presence. The asthmatic hot water radiator that stands sentinel around the perimeter of the room shudders into operation in an agonizing series of coughs and wheezes. The spasms build to a clattering crescendo, then fade away. The noise blankets our silences. We sit cocooned in our pockets of grief, the edges touching.

Sometimes sorrow is best shared in silence, in the still acknowledgment of pain and searing loss. I am not good at silences, but Norman taught me the beauty of stillness in his time with us. He was a man who knew, more than any man I have ever known, how to be still before his God. He was a man who knew, even in suffering, how to abide.

Across from me, Sue holds her husband's hand. She and Jeff will have to leave within hours to prepare to travel to the bedside of Jeff's mother, who is awaiting critical surgery. Sue's grief is for what was, for what is, and for what is to come. Within the hour, she will kiss her father's face for the last time this side of heaven.

Beside me, Dan's chin quivers with the reality of the loss that hovers on the horizon, the loss that he will face without his sister at his side. Grief binds us in our shared pain, our shared memories, and our shared love.

This hour is our gift to one another. We have ministered and poured out all that we have in the past days. We have planned and prepared, prayed and praised. Now it is time for tears . . . and silence.

I nestle into Dan's chest and feel the soft shudder of his breathing as I clench my eyes tight and listen for the footsteps of the doctor. But the footsteps do not come, and I breathe deeply and pull Dan's arm close around my shoulder.

One at a time, I pull down the photos in my memory and finger them gently, stroking the things most precious to me and reminding myself why they are so dear. A family Christmas. The look on Norman's face when he spoke of his children and grandchildren. His head bent low over his Bible in prayer.

I pull Dan's arm closer, knowing that eternity has touched us all in this hour—the past touching the present and transporting us into the reality of our future hope.

Our joy is not joy in a life well lived. It is joy in the assurance of a life that lives on. It is the heritage of a godly father and his most precious gift, the hope of eternal life—a hope that binds our hearts even in grief.

Dear heavenly Father, You know the depth of my grief for my loved one, the searing sorrow that I feel over his loss. Even knowing the hope of heaven, Jesus wept with heartrending sorrow over the loss of His loved ones in death. Lord, let me find solace in my time of tears as I mourn the loss of my loved one. Let me recognize that tears are a gift and that You have given them to me as a means of expressing my deep love for those I care for. Father, help me not to become consumed by my grief, but to use it as a stepping-stone toward restoration, for You do not intend to leave me scarred and torn. Pour out Your sustaining grace on my hurting heart, dear Lord, and bear me up at this difficult time.

IN WHAT WAYS HAS weeping been a blessing to you? How has it helped you to heal? How have your tears helped others in their mourning?

There is a time for everything,
and a season for every activity under heaven . . .
a time to mourn and a time to dance.

ECCLESIASTES 3:1, 4

Dan and I are returning home for our first night of rest
in weeks. The hospice staff has assured us that his father
is sleeping comfortably and is expected to remain so for
the night. We have been with him continuously for almost
three weeks, and his condition has stabilized with the new
drugs the hospice team has put into place. They assure us
that they will call us at any sign of change, and we reluctantly decide to go home. We know that the days ahead
will grow more difficult, and we leave knowing that we will
need every ounce of rest we can store up.

I sigh and pull Dan's hand into my own as we drive. It
is as though some unseen force has pushed our heads un-
derwater these past weeks and our lungs are at their burst-

ing point. We need a fresh intake of air, and I gaze at the winter fields to remind myself that the world beyond the confines of our loss is still there.

The ride home is quiet. Sue and Jeff have left for their long drive back to New York. The good-byes were wrenching but sweet. Sue is in my thoughts as Dan and I drive the seven miles to our home. I cannot imagine placing a last kiss upon my father's brow, then stepping from the room where I know he will die. Sue did it with the same dignity, simplicity, and sweetness with which she has done all things. She is a woman after God's own heart.

At home, Mom and Dad await. They have been housebound since Norman's illness, with few outings and few distractions. The rare times that I have had away from the hospital and the veteran's home, I have taken them out for lunches or run errands with them to assuage my guilt for leaving them alone for days on end. Dad has been graciously understanding, helping with the laundry and loading and unloading the dishwasher. It is his love language, spoken in silence and quiet awkwardness.

Dan and I arrive home and cross the threshold of grief and despair into the realm of the surreal. Dad sits at the kitchen table in his dungarees and a blue T-shirt with a kitten on it. He is eating Swedish pancakes and listening to the shiny new radio he recently purchased at Dollar General for five bucks. The volume is cranked to somewhere just below the sound barrier and salsa music fills the air. Although Dad speaks not a word of Spanish, he has recently developed an affinity for a Mexican radio station.

Mom hovers near the table in her pink robe and slippers. The snaps are done up katty-wompus, with the bottom hiked up somewhere near her waist, giving her a somewhat come-hither look. She waves at me across the room, like she is getting ready to climb aboard a bus for a ride into the city. The look on her face tells me that at this moment I may be her sister Erma or the muffin man, but I am not her daughter.

From the living room, Animal Planet is blaring. The narrator is reciting fascinating statistics about giraffe behavior. His words drift into the kitchen, wafting over the top of the salsa music. "Giraffes produce the loudest burps in the animal kingdom, at 128 decibels."

I turn to Dan, my eyes wide.

"No one has my life," I say. "No one even believes me when I tell them about it."

There is only one possible thing to do. I step toward my mother, grab her by the hand, and twirl her around the kitchen in a few tentative dance steps. They are the best efforts of a brain-damaged Baptist and an eighty-three-year-old Alzheimer's sufferer. But they are my best offering of joy in a moment when I could have chosen despair. And in God's eyes, I believe, Fred and Ginger pale by comparison.

Father, help me to claim joy in the moments when it arises. May I seek it and claim it as my own in the midst of suffering and sorrow. May I have eyes to see beauty even in the pain and laughter even in the heartache.

WHAT GIFTS OF JOY has God graced you with? Where have you found joy in pain?

_____

_____

_____

_____

_____

_____

_____

_____

_____

_____

*But Moses said, "O Lord, please send someone else to do it." . . .
[And God said,] "He will speak to the people for you,
and it will be as if he were your mouth."*

EXODUS 4:13, 16

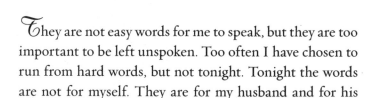

They are not easy words for me to speak, but they are too important to be left unspoken. Too often I have chosen to run from hard words, but not tonight. Tonight the words are not for myself. They are for my husband and for his father.

"Have you said everything that you need to say?"

Dan and I sit huddled in our loveseat in a darkened living room, my head resting upon his chest. He has just returned from a grueling school board meeting that required his oversight, and it is approaching midnight. His eyes wear a look of weariness that runs clear through to his soul. The past two weeks of split shifts at his father's bedside have drained him past the point of exhaustion. The edges of his heart have worn raw as he's watched his father slip away in bits and pieces.

The silence is prolonged as the tears course down his face. I trace the tracks lightly with my fingers.

"No. After seven years, I haven't found time to say it all." The words catch in his throat.

I take my husband's hand and draw him to his feet.

"Then you'll say it tonight."

He hears the urgency in my voice and knows without asking what I am saying. The nurses have called to report that his father is slipping into a coma.

"We need to go, Dan."

We stand frozen in the darkness, knowing that our next steps will move us further down the path toward his father's death.

We make our journey in silence, driving through the chill winter air misted with finely powdered snow. At the veteran's home the elevator to the third floor carries us to the familiar corridor we have walked for eleven months. The small, private room we have been granted by hospice has become sacred ground.

Dan settles quietly in an overstuffed chair left behind by a former resident. He angles toward his father's body as he speaks his words of love.

Childhood memories. Favorite vacations. Words of honor.

His father's eyes stare straight ahead, unblinking. Occasionally the flicker of an eyebrow tells us that he hears.

Dan's tears flow freely as he thanks his father for his most precious memory—the gift of leading him to the Lord as a child. He weeps as he describes the day, the hour.

The eyebrow flickers once again.

We read letters of love and honor from his grandchildren and from Sue. With our words, we bathe our dying precious one's heart in truth and love. The words bathe our hearts as well.

In those moments when death lingers at the doorway and we are allowed to say good-bye, we are blessed. Words of parting can be draped in ceremony or stated in simplicity, but they are God's gift for both the dying and the bereaved. And sometimes the greatest gift we can offer is to help someone share those words with the ones they love.

Dear God, give me boldness to speak words of blessing to those I love and care for. Don't let me make the mistake of denying words of grace, forgiveness, mercy, and compassion. Help me to speak the difficult things that would bless my loved one, to grace them with a love offering of words. Grant me wisdom in knowing when to speak and what to speak. May the words of my mouth be acceptable in Your sight.

WHAT WORDS OF comfort, forgiveness, affirmation, or grace would bless the heart of your loved one? If you knew that today were your last day with them, what message would you want to share with them?

_____

_____

_____

_____

_____

_____

_____

_____

_____

_____

"There is no one like the God of Jeshurun,
who rides on the heavens to help you
and on the clouds in his majesty.
The eternal God is your refuge,
and underneath are the everlasting arms."

DEUTERONOMY 33:26–27

𝒟an's call comes at eight in the morning. His father is gone. He slipped away peacefully in the early morning hours as Dan dozed at his bedside.

A sense of urgency washes over me, an overwhelming need to be beside my husband in this moment, pressing into his solid frame. But I am home, details pulling at my mind as I lay the phone back on the nightstand.

Dad has heard the phone ring and is waiting in the hallway. I breathe a quick prayer that Mom is still asleep and am rewarded to see her thin figure still shrouded beneath the bedcovers. I assure him that friends will bring supper by, but I don't know when we will be home because I'm not sure what we will do next. Tightness grips my chest as I think of a thousand things I should have done before the inevitability of this moment, and I'm suddenly angry at myself for not having done them sooner. But the most important thing is to be with Dan, to hold my husband.

I don't remember the ride to the veteran's home or the elevator or the nurses who greeted me in the hallway. My only memory is of the silence of the room and Dan sitting at the foot of the bed, his hand resting lightly on the pale blue blanket—and of the loss etched upon his face.

It is my turn to speak my last good-bye. I stroke Norman's arm and tell him how loved he was, how honored we were to have shared his life, how we treasured his prayers and his love for us. Dan and I hold each other and weep. Then we gather the pictures and photo albums, slip them into the bags I have brought, and move quickly into the hallway.

The door swings shut softly behind us. And at that moment, something deep within my body that has kept vigil for weeks swings softly shut as well.

The elevator descends to ground level, and with each passing floor, the strength that has sustained me for the past weeks ebbs from my body. It's as though I am shriveling from within. Before Dan and I exit the building, exhaustion overtakes me with a stranglehold so intense that I double over. Numbness settles over my thoughts, and I am unable to speak. Dan reaches for my hand, and I burst into spasms of uncontrolled sobs. I cannot formulate a single coherent thought.

A single phrase forms on my lips, and I repeat it over and over as Dan drives the back roads toward home.

"I'm just so tired . . . so tired . . ."

I'm wracked by guilt to say such a selfish thing in the starkest moment of my husband's loss. The sobs hijack my body once again, and shame washes over me. I tell myself that this is not how a spiritual wife supports her husband in his time of grief. This is not how Elda Ann or Mona would act. They are the "godly" women in my life whom I have placed on pedestals of my own making. I tell myself that they would hold their husband's hands and quote Scripture. That they would be strong. I can barely remember my name.

Then the words of a good friend remind me of the truth. I am strong, and I have been strong in the power God has provided to sustain me through days and nights of comfort at my dying father-in-law's bedside. My parents have been safe and secure in my home, loved and provided for throughout it all. I have held my husband's hand and stood at his side. I have faithfully ministered to a dying loved one's body and spirit for days, weeks, and years, and I am exhausted. I need to allow myself to be restored.

For the next two days, I devote myself to rest, taking every available moment to sleep, to cloister myself from intrusion. In life, in death, in restoration God sustains. And in the moments when our strength fails, He bears us up and carries us.

> *Precious Lord, take my hand, lead me on, help me stand. I am tired, I am weak, I am worn. Through the storm, through the night, lead me on to the light. Take my hand, precious Lord, lead me home.*
>
> *Father, give me Your strength when all strength is gone. Give me Your hope when all I see is despair. Give me rest in the midst of chaos. Bear me up and carry me, Dear Lord, for You alone are my refuge.*

GOD DESIRES FOR YOU to find rest. In what ways can you build physical rest into your life? In what ways can you build spiritual rest into your life? How are you already doing that, and what steps do you need to take to do it in ways that will give you even greater refreshment?

_____

_____

_____

_____

_____

In this you greatly rejoice,
though now for a little while you may have had to
suffer grief in all kinds of trials.
These have come so that your faith—of greater worth than gold,
which perishes even though refined by fire—
may be proved genuine and may result in praise, glory and
honor when Jesus Christ is revealed.

1 PETER 1:6–7

The harsh rattle of Norman's breathing is stilled, and the quiet timbre of his voice is now a memory. Grief for his loss crescendos and recedes as we prepare for his funeral.

My heart is fragile as I dress my mother for the service. In Norman's final days I shopped for an outfit and accessories that I hoped would accommodate Mom's need for comfort, warmth, and ease in dressing, yet fulfill her love for wearing soft pastels. Even the necklace and earrings were purchased with a desire to honor her lifelong delight in dressing up and looking beautiful.

But Mom can no longer see the intentions of my heart. Her body can only perceive its own weariness and confusion. On the day when I desire most to be met with her sweet smile, I am met with the second grief of her anger.

I grieve afresh for loss cocooned within loss, for abandonment in my time of pain. This grief has taken me to a new place of suffering. Were it not for God, it would take me to despair. I grieve tonight for the loss of a loved one—not to physical death, but to love and nurture that have slipped away into the night.

What do we do when we do not get what we want, when our intentions are misjudged, our hearts misread? What do we do when in our most painful seasons of loss, when we long to be met with outstretched hands and loving arms, we are met with something less?

We do what Christ did. We choose love—loving God with all our heart, soul, and mind, and loving others as ourselves.

It's impossible to say that we love God without reflecting that love in selfless devotion to others. So we choose words that preserve life. We choose actions that preserve life. We choose attitudes that preserve life. We do all that is within our power to preserve the welfare of those who have wounded us. And we choose to love as Christ loved:

unconditionally, unequivocally, and unreservedly, without regard for what will be given in return.

This is the truth of the double-love command, and it is central to caregiving, whether that care be for our children, our spouse, our church family, our colleagues, or the world around us.

Culture teaches us that pain means entitlement. Scripture teaches us that pain means provision.

Culture teaches us to stand up for ourselves. Scripture teaches us to lay down our lives for others.

Culture teaches us to demand what is rightfully ours. Scripture teaches us to give up what was never ours in the first place.

For most of my life I have fought against silences, for they expose the empty places within me—black holes of contentment, complacency, pride, fear. But I am learning that in the silences I can hear the still small whispers I have kept so long at bay. I have found that pain and silence are God's hearing aids.

Tonight I grieve a double grief, for Norman and for the pain of a wounded, misread heart. But there is peace in knowing that grief will mold me if I am willing to conform my heart to the pressure of God's hands. My prayer is that He will speak to me in the silence and use the pain to show me the black holes of contentment, complacency, pride, and fear that lie so deep within me. I pray that even in my moment of deepest pain and grief, I might learn to bring God praise, glory, and honor.

> *Dear Father, You know that when I am hurt, my instinct is to protect myself and to lash out. You know that when I am wounded I am at my weakest, but You have told us that in our weakness, You are our strength. Father God, I commit my heart to obedience in the double-love command—to love You with all my heart, soul, and mind, and to love my neighbor in that same way, even when it is painful and requires sacrifice. Help me learn to love unconditionally, without regard for what is given in return. Expose the black holes of contentment, complacency, pride, and fear in my life. I pray that even in my pain and grief, I might bring You praise and glory and honor.*

WHEN IS IT MOST difficult for you to practice the double-love command? In what areas of your life is God asking you to let go of selfishness, pride, complacency, and fear?

_____

_____

_____

_____

_____

_____

_____

[Your beauty] should be that of your inner self,
the unfading beauty of a gentle and quiet spirit,
which is of great worth in God's sight.

1 PETER 3:4

$\mathcal{W}$e have settled into the front pews of Norman's home church in Rochester, New York, after greeting the dozens of people who have come through the door—people who have grown old in the twenty or thirty years since we have last seen them. We are content to be oblivious to our own gray hair, wrinkles, and saggage. We have introduced our children and walked people through the display of mementos and photographs honoring Norman's life. He has come home a final time to be buried near his beloved wife, Marian. Friends and relatives offer memories and remembrances, and we embrace each one. They are gifts to our family—flashes of the past, like camera bursts of light on Norman's life.

The pastor begins the memorial service with Scripture and prayer and offers the microphone to anyone wishing to offer a word of tribute for Norman. Old friends speak. Fellow Bible college students. Church members. Then, from the rear of the church, a man stands and speaks.

"No one here knows who I am. I don't know any of you, and I don't go to this church. I read the obituary in the paper and knew I had to come.

"I don't think I ever spoke a word to Norman Beach, but I worked with him years ago when I was pretty rough around the edges. Back then, eight o'clock would roll around, and all us guys would still be standing around drinking coffee and talking, but Norman would be diving into work. At noon, he'd get out his Bible and read while he ate while we were loud and carrying on. He never said a lot. He just did his work and read his Bible and was kind to people. When it was quitting time, we were always ready to clock out early, and Norman was always willing to work a little late.

"About five years after Norman left Kodak, I got saved and found out what it meant to know Jesus Christ. I've never been able to give my testimony without mentioning Norm Beach. He's the first person who showed me what a Christian was supposed to be like."

We never got the chance to find out who the man was. He slipped out before any of our family had a chance to speak to him.

The last day Dad Beach was with us, as he lay in a coma, we read to him from his favorite daily devotional. The selection that day was about God's perspective on unremarkable lives. It seemed poignantly appropriate. The last years of Norman's life were lived in relative solitude. Social interaction, even with family, grew increasingly difficult for him as he aged. He chose, in his final years, the solace of his room and the comfort of prayer and Scripture. Yet he was never in solitude. He sought the continual presence of God.

Sometimes life leaves us feeling that our tasks are mundane, even tedious, that our days are repetitive and have no significance. But Dad Beach knew the truth—that no moment lived for God is an insignificant moment. The beauty of his spirit was just as evident on the floor of the factory as it was when he was sharing the gospel as a missionary. He found joy in serving God in the way he ate his lunch and interacted with coworkers. His gentle and quiet spirit were of incomparable beauty.

Today, as I spoon food into my mother's mouth, I pray that I do it with beauty. As I remind my father how to interact with her, I pray that I do it with gentleness and grace. I pray that in watching me, others will see what a true Christian is supposed to be like, even in the simple things.

Dear heavenly Father, there are so many days my life feels mundane and tedious. Thank You for giving significance to every second, every moment, because You see all that I do. May all that I do be done for Your glory. Father, grow me in my inner self. I know this won't come easily, but I desire the unfading beauty of a gentle and quiet spirit. Grow me into the person You desire me to be. Thank You for seeing not only who I am, but who You intend me to be.

WHAT THINGS OF eternal significance have you given to God today? In what areas of your spirit do you think God may want to grow you? Has He already spoken to you about His desires for your spiritual growth? How can you move ahead toward this desire?

_____

_____

_____

_____

_____

_____

_____

_____

_____

_____

*"In the future, when your children ask you,
'What do these stones mean?' tell them
that the flow of the Jordan was cut off before
the ark of the covenant of the Lord . . .
These stones are to be a memorial
to the people of Israel forever."*

JOSHUA 4:6–7

We have gathered at the small country cemetery near
Rochester, New York, where Norman will be interred beside his dear Marian. Jessica and Nathan hover near Dan
and me as we stand beside the hearse, waiting for a few
remaining family members to gather. I am comforted by
the presence of my children. They have never seen their
grandmother's grave. I know that it is unlikely that they
will stand in this place again.

The weather is damp and cold, and I bury my hand
within Dan's and lean into his side. I lay my head against

his arm as I watch the honor guard assemble. The men lining up behind a bank of gravestones are aged. They are gray-haired or balding, gnarled and limping. But the men I see are uniformed heroes, soldiers who gripped their sweethearts in their arms and said good-bye when the world was teetering on the edge of a great abyss, men whose sacrifice helped keep it from falling in.

Behind us, a royal blue awning has been erected above a casket draped in an American flag. We stand in silence as the head of the honor guard speaks words of condolence for our family on behalf of the military. Then we take our places in the chairs, and family members share words of honor and remembrance.

Dan moves to the graveside and speaks. His hand rests lightly the casket. His final caress.

When his tribute has ended, Dan sits beside me once again. I reach for his hand, but the gunfire startles me. With the first of the volleys, I jump. I hold my breath with the second and third, and listen as the shots echo through the morning air.

The two youngest members of the honor guard move into place and gently slip the flag from the coffin, as a World War II veteran intones the significance of the flag-folding ceremony in solemn tones.

I am unprepared for the beauty and precision of the choreography that unfolds before my eyes. The white gloves hover and flitter, fingers precisely aligned and angled. Each movement is an exercise in beauty and grace. When the flag is folded, the young soldier dips into his pocket and pulls out three bullets, aligned between his fingers with exacting precision. The voice of the older veteran explains their significance.

Honor. The first bullet is tucked deeply into the recesses of the flag as the merits of honor are explained.

Duty. The second bullet is buried in the flag as the quality of duty is presented.

Love. The third bullet is hidden within the flag as a second honor guardsman holds the flag firmly within his hands.

With a final flourish the flag is presented to the family as a symbol of honor from the military to the family of a soldier who has faithfully served. As the ceremony of honor ends, we linger for a moment under the balm of its touch.

This ceremony, like all ceremonies, is a picture of purpose. God knew this when He established ceremonies in the Old Testament. They help us see beyond ourselves to significance that extends beyond the temporal and the superficial. Ceremonies create a heritage for our children and help us remember what God has done, help us see the greater purposes of pain and suffering.

We play an integral role in an eternal story. This is the

ultimate hope in our calling. It is the ultimate purpose in our life and gives us the strength to put our roots down deeply in the face of difficulty and trials.

> *Dear heavenly Father, thank You for allowing me to play a role in Your eternal story. May I put my roots down deeply in the face of difficulty and trials. Thank You for the gift of ceremony. Help me to look for opportunity to create ceremonies for my family to help them remember and commemorate Your provisions and blessings in life. May I always be searching for ways to praise and honor You and to remember all the blessings that You have poured out upon me.*

WHAT CEREMONIES of thanksgiving could you create for your family or loved ones? What role are you playing in God's eternal story? A role of encouragement? A role of provision? A role of extending Jesus' love?

_____

_____

_____

_____

_____

_____

_____

_____

So we fix our eyes not on what is seen,
but on what is unseen.
For what is seen is temporary,
but what is unseen is eternal.

2 CORINTHIANS 4:18

$\mathcal{S}$ome miracles come swaddled and cradled in a manger.

Others come unfurled in sweeping clouds and blazing chariots.

My mother sits beside me, a miracle softly draped in a gauzy green pantsuit and pearls. My father settles beside her, cupping her shoulders in his outstretched arm and holding one hand lightly in his own. His posture declares to those present his devotion to his own bride. They have just been ushered down the aisle of the church for my nephew Brian's wedding. My mother, smiling and nodding sweetly, could not grace the room with more decorum if she were the Queen Mother herself.

It is a miracle I had not even dared to pray for, especially when Brian informed me that both sets of grandparents would be asked to stand during the ceremony to participate in a corporate moment of blessing. Although I recognized the beauty of the concept, the practicality of the matter terrified me. Deep down, I doubted that Mom would be capable of handling the ride across the state, the unfamiliar environment, the dozens of friends and relatives who would greet her, much less the challenge of late afternoon and a role in the ceremony.

I sit sandwiched between Dan and my parents as my mother nestles into my father's shoulder and the wedding video begins. Her eyes shift to the screen as images of Brian and Christy's childhoods flicker before us, larger than life. I point and whisper, narrating as scenes of children and grandchildren flash in frozen clips of memory.

A moment later, music begins—strains of a song that chronicles the journey of life, of childhood, of growing up, of meeting and falling in love, of growing old together and remaining faithful until the end.

I slide my fingers into the hand of the weeping man who sits beside me, who has honored and cherished me in sickness and in health and never wavered. The words and music speak a truth deep within us, and in that moment my eyes close in a prayer of thanks.

Beside me, my father strokes my mother's hand. In a few

moments the two will rise, side by side, and he will speak words of blessing upon the bride and groom. Then they will sit, together, as they have always done, until it is time for my father to lead my mother away.

In front of me, my sister-in-law Sheryl waits for her son to emerge from the groom's door to await his bride. My brother Paul will walk beside him as one of his groomsmen.

The circle of life plays out before our eyes as generations link hands, whisper blessings, embrace.

But like the groom who sees only the veiled face of his bride beneath a swath of white until the moment she truly is his own, we see only the shape and the shadow of our sovereign destinies in our fleeting moments here on earth. What appears to us as the reality of life is only preparation for what is to come. The mysteries of suffering and pain will one day be erased when Jesus Christ unlocks the doors to our past, present, and future hope. There we will see the part that we played in His sovereign plan for the universe and for all time.

So, while we are grateful for the miracles that gift our days, for the luxury of laughter, the fragrance of family, we know that what we see now is temporary. We look beyond the veil to the day when God will reveal all things.

This is our blessed hope.

Gracious Lord and Master, I look longingly for the day when I will see You face to face and all pain will be erased. You alone see my destiny from beginning to end and the role that I play in Your eternal plan. Thank You for loving me, even in my unloveliness. May I seek after You with passion that burns from within me and drives out all fear and doubt. Today I choose to walk in the joy of the blessed hope of eternal life that You have given me as Your chosen child, dear Father.

WHAT DOES IT mean to shift your focus from things that are "seen" to things that are "unseen"? How does knowing that God is using you to carry out a specific aspect of His plan in history change your perspective about your life?

_____

_____

_____

_____

_____

_____

_____

_____

_____

_____

ACKNOWLEDGMENTS

 $\mathcal{T}$ his book was a journey, and I would like to thank the many people who have made it possible. First and foremost, my husband Dan, whose endless encouragement has been my greatest gift. You are the love of my life, and I am blessed beyond measure.

To my children, Jessica and Nathan, who are my heroes, and who have taken on their faith like spiritual skydivers plunging in a freefall toward earth, leaving me breathless and with palpitations staring from the safety of the plane.

To my brother Paul and his dear wife Sheryl, hearts of my own heart. You have given above measure, pressed down and poured out upon the lives of our family. And to your children, Andy, Keri, and Brian, and Brian's wife Christy, who have blessed our family in giving of themselves and in being the amazing people God created them to be.

To Sue and Jeff, Dan's sister and brother-in-law, who are the epitome of grace and love. Thank you for years of unwavering support and devotion to Dad Beach and to us. And to Erin and Chris, for showering Grandpa Beach with letters and pictures of those beautiful babies in his final years. Nothing blessed his heart more.

Most of all to our parents—Paul and Phyllis Burke, and Norman and Marian Beach—for their years of devotion as godly parents who sought to raise their children in the nurture and admonition of the Lord. You embraced us with love, support, and encouragement that few families know.

I would also like to thank the wild and wondrous women of the Guild—Ann Byle, Lorilee Craker, Tracy Groot, Jen Abbas, Julie Johnson, Angela Blycker, Katrina De Man, Alison Hodgson, Sharon Carrns, and Cynthia Beach. You embraced me as a writer before I dared to embrace myself.

I am forever indebted to the teaching ministry of Blythefield Hills Baptist Church in Grand Rapids, Michigan. Their pastoring, small group, and discipleship ministries have impacted both my life and Dan's life at our core, and we are deeply grateful. To my accountability sisters, thank you for your devotion and commitment to my heart. In you I am blessed.

NOTE TO THE READER

The publisher invites you to share your response to the message of this book by writing Discovery House Publishers, P.O. Box 3566, Grand Rapids, MI 49501, U.S.A. For information about other Discovery House books, music, videos, or DVDs, contact us at the same address or call 1-800-653-8333. Find us on the Internet at http://www.dhp.org/ or send e-mail to books@dhp.org.